# GREENPRINT

# GREENPRINT

## *A New Approach to Cooperation on Climate Change*

Aaditya Mattoo

Arvind Subramanian

CENTER FOR GLOBAL DEVELOPMENT
*Washington, D.C.*

*Library of Congress Cataloging-in-Publication data*
Mattoo, Aaditya.
  Greenprint : a new approach to cooperation on climate change / Aaditya Mattoo and Arvind Subramanian.
     p.    cm.
  Includes bibliographical references.
  ISBN 978-1-933286-67-9 (pbk. : alk. paper)
  1. Economic development—Environmental aspects. 2. Developing countries—Economic conditions. 3. Climate change mitigation—International cooperation.
I. Subramanian, Arvind. II. Title.
  HD75.6.M396 2012
  363.738'74—dc23                          2012040591

9 8 7 6 5 4 3 2 1

Printed on acid-free paper

*Greenprint: A New Approach to Cooperation on Climate Change* may be ordered from:
Brookings Institution Press, c/o HFS, P.O. Box 50370, Baltimore, MD 21211-4370
Tel.: 800/537-5487; 410/516-6956; Fax: 410/516-6998
www.brookings.edu/press

Chapter 2 is adapted from Aaditya Mattoo and Arvind Subramanian, "Equity in Climate Change: An Analytical Review," *World Development* 40(6): 1083–97. © 2011 Elsevier Ltd. All rights reserved.

Chapter 3 is adapted from Nancy Birdsall and Arvind Subramanian, "Energy Needs and Efficiency, Not Emissions: Re-framing the Climate Change Narrative," CGD Working Paper 187 (Washington: Center for Global Development, 2009). © 2009 Center for Global Development. Some rights reserved.

Chapter 4 is adapted from Aaditya Mattoo, Arvind Subramanian, Dominique van der Mensbrugghe, and Jianwu He, "Can Global Decarbonization Inhibit Developing Country Indistrialization?" *The World Bank Economic Review* 26(2): 269–319. © 2011 Aaditya Mattoo. All rights reserved.

Chapter 5 is adapted from Aaditya Mattoo, Arvind Subramanian, Dominique van der Mensbrugghe, and Jianwu He, "Reconciling Climate Change and Trade Policy," CGD Working Paper 189 (Washington: Center for Global Development, 2009). © 2009 Center for Global Development. Some rights reserved. An adaptation is forthcoming as Aaditya Mattoo, Arvind Subramanian, Dominique van der Mensbrugghe, and Jianwu He, "Trade Effects of Alternative Carbon Border-Tax Schemes," *Review of World Economics*.

# Contents

# Foreword

To delay acting on climate change is to run great risks of fundamentally rewriting the relationship between human beings and the planet. The risks of inaction, in the lifetime of children born today, include the potential movement of hundreds of millions of people—possibly billions—with devastating effects on livelihoods and living standards across the world. Yet discussion and action in much of the rich world is atrophied, and in emerging-market and developing countries there is concern that action on climate change will impede the battle against poverty in the next few decades.

There is a way forward: we must understand that the alternative low-carbon growth paths can be very attractive and that the transition to them from high-carbon growth paths will be full of discovery. The only path that is sustainable is the medium-term path of growth and poverty reduction. The issues of climate change, growth, and poverty reduction are inextricably intertwined. Failure to manage climate change will undermine development and poverty reduction; failure to promote development and reduce poverty will further exacerbate climate change.

A new energy–industrial revolution is needed. Realizing this transformation will require both leadership and collaboration. It now looks as if that leadership will have to come from the emerging-market countries and the developing world. But the rich cannot retreat from their responsibility to help with both resources and technologies and to take strong action to reduce their emissions. It is time to break out of the old "cash for cuts" and zero-sum approaches that have driven earlier discussions and models of international negotiations on climate change. That realization has begun in Cancun and Durban, with the ideas of "equitable access to sustainable development" and the increasing commitment of China, India, and others to new technologies.

It is the emerging and developing nations that are undergoing economic growth and thus emission growth, and these countries are also the ones hit earliest and hardest by climate change—although we are all at great risk. It is time to accelerate action, and to do that we must look to the developing world to chart a path and to the rich world to both act strongly in support and share leadership through its own actions and examples. This important book, in its treatment of international action on climate change, sets forth a detailed and sensible way forward. It should be read by all of those who are involved in economic development and international action on climate change.

Lord Nicholas Stern
*London*
*November 2012*

# Preface

The Center for Global Development focuses on policies and actions of the rich and powerful that spur or impede the pace of development for the world's poor. Aid, debt relief, open markets for developing-country exports, and more open borders to allow migration: these are widely seen as "development" issues. They generate, if not consensus, then at least a shared framework within which debate takes place.

From its early years, CGD has been concerned with adding climate change to that framework. Senior fellow emeritus David Wheeler has published more than a dozen CGD working papers on climate and is the architect of two emissions-mapping tools, Carbon Monitoring for Action (CARMA), which tracks power plants, and Forest Monitoring for Action (FORMA), which uses satellite data to track tropical deforestation. His more recent work estimates the vulnerability of 233 countries to three major effects of climate change (weather-related disasters, sea-level rise, and reduced agricultural productivity). William Cline's 2007 book, *Global Warming and Agriculture: Impact Estimates by Country* (CGD and the Peterson Institute for International Economics), revealed the stakes for developing countries: a projected 45 percent reduction in agricultural productivity in India and similar losses in much of sub-Saharan Africa.

Climate change is a natural addition to CGD's work because poor people in the developing world are feeling its impacts first and worst in some considerable part because high-income countries are responsible for the bulk of greenhouse gas emissions causing climate change. But climate change is also very different because the issue is no longer one of rich versus poor. Some developing countries are now major emitters, and the developing world accounts for more than half of all current greenhouse gases. To be effective, responses to climate change must address developing countries' needs, including their right to development, but developing countries are now so big that they must also actively contribute to remedies. In other words, climate change requires a genuinely cooperative solution, involving rich and poor, in contrast to CGD's "first-generation" issues, which focused on rich-country actions.

*Greenprint*, by Aaditya Mattoo and Arvind Subramanian, is the first major piece of work that addresses the key challenge of global cooperation in the new world of changing economic and fiscal strengths among poor and rich countries. In this new world, the role of India, China, and other rising emerging markets will be key to forging cooperation on climate change. Indeed, Mattoo and Subramanian raise the question whether there needs to be a serious role reversal when it comes to climate change. Why should the West necessarily take the lead when the issues are greater for developing countries? Indeed, is it clear today which country is the real recalcitrant on climate change? Isn't the current approach in which the rich offer compensation to the poor overtaken by the fact that the rich world is economically weak and debt-addled? Mustn't we now also think of ways in which countries like China might create healthy pressure on the United States to take action to prevent climate change? If radically green technology is the only way to reconcile climate change goals with development aspirations, shouldn't all countries contribute to technology generation and dissemination?

These are just a few of the new and rich questions to which *Greenprint* provides answers. Some are controversial, and some might be politically unlikely. But the freshness of the approach and the innovative solutions in *Greenprint* are sure to generate a new round of debate, not just on climate change but on international cooperation more broadly in this new and changing world.

Nancy Birdsall
*President*
*Center for Global Development*

# 1

# A "Greenprint" for International Cooperation on Climate Change

The difficulty lies not so much in developing new ideas as in escaping from old ones.
—John Maynard Keynes, *The General Theory of Employment Interest and Money*

International negotiations on climate change have been dogged by mutual recriminations between rich and poor countries, constricted by the zero-sum arithmetic of a shrinking global carbon budget, and overtaken by shifts in economic and hence bargaining power between industrialized and developing countries. We call these three factors, respectively, the "narrative," "adding-up," and "new world" problems. Given these factors, the wonder is not the current impasse. It is rather the idea that progress might be possible at all.

But there is a way forward. It requires a radical change in the approach to cooperation on climate change. We propose a "Greenprint for cooperation" that calls for a major role reversal between the developed and developing countries, a shift in emphasis from emissions reduction to technology generation, and a radical reconfiguring of contributions by individual countries.

First, instead of waiting for the industrial countries to lead, the large "dynamic emerging economies"—China, India, Brazil, and Indonesia, hereafter referred to as DEEs—must assume that mantle, offering contributions of their own and prodding the reluctant West, especially the United States, into action. This role reversal would be consistent with the fact that the stakes in the near to medium term are much greater for the DEEs than for today's rich countries.

1

Second, instead of focusing exclusively on emissions cuts by all, which would imply either unacceptable cuts in consumption in rich countries or poor countries' having to forgo the rudiments of modernity, the emphasis must be on technology generation. This would allow greater consumption and production possibilities for all countries while respecting the global emissions budget, about 750 gigatons of carbon dioxide over the next forty years, that is dictated by the climate change goal of keeping average temperature rise below 2 degrees centigrade.

Third, instead of basing cooperation on the old "cash-for-cuts" approach—not feasible today because the economically enfeebled rich are in no position to offer meaningful compensation to poorer countries in return for cuts in their carbon emissions—all major emitters, the rich and the dynamic poor alike, must make contributions, calibrated in magnitude and form to development levels and prospects. "From each, according to its ability, and to each, the common good of planetary survival" might be a characterization of contribution and reward in this new approach.

In this chapter we spell out how our proposed Greenprint would work, but first we explore the three major problems and why so little progress has taken place to date. We end with thoughts on the plausibility that this Greenprint can provide a basis for progress.

## The Cancun, Copenhagen, and Durban "Deals"

These seem unusually inauspicious times to discuss, let alone yearn for, international cooperation to address the problem of climate change. After all, the three most recent summits held under the UN Framework Convention on Climate Change (UNFCCC)—Copenhagen in 2009, Cancun in 2010, and Durban in 2011—have come and gone. They, especially Durban, have offered only a thin reed of hope based on nothing more than promises to make more meaningful promises later, rather than on concrete commitments to act now.

To the glass-half-fullers, the Copenhagen summit had notable successes:

—It moved climate change up to the top of the political agenda.
—It took several significant steps, including spelling out the goal of limiting global warming to 2 degrees centigrade.

—It called for arrangements to mobilize $100 billion a year by 2020 to help developing countries adapt to climate change, that is, to adjust to the warming that does occur despite mitigation efforts.

—It established an advisory group to look at financing options.[1]

But to the glass-half-emptyers, the meeting was notable for what did not happen:

—There was no agreement on binding emissions cuts and only promises of best efforts at the national level; indeed, no aggregate emissions target was set, not even for 2050.

—There was no commitment to provide public resources to the poorest countries, only broad statements of intent to provide international assistance.

—There was no agreement on international monitoring, reporting, and verification, but some willingness to countenance international consultation.

—There was no mechanism for reducing emissions from deforestation and forest degradation, although there was some recognition of the "need" for the "immediate establishment of a mechanism."

—And there was no discussion of international trade in emissions rights.

In Cancun a year later, expectations were so low that what did occur was an upside surprise. Although there was still no agreement on binding emissions reductions, the Cancun summit did lead to emissions reduction pledges from both developed and developing countries, involving all of the major economies and the largest emitters—China, the United States, the European Union, India, and Brazil. The agreements included a mechanism to track countries' progress in meeting those commitments and a review of the adequacy of the commitments in meeting long-term global emissions reduction goals. And they established a number of mechanisms and institutions to help accelerate emissions cuts and protect vulnerable countries, such as a Green Climate Fund, a global network of climate-related technology experts, an adaptation framework, and a strategy for tackling deforestation.[1]

1. Houser (2010).

**FIGURE 1-1.  Pledges to Reduce Emissions Are Woefully Inadequate: Projected GHG Emissions under Different Scenarios**

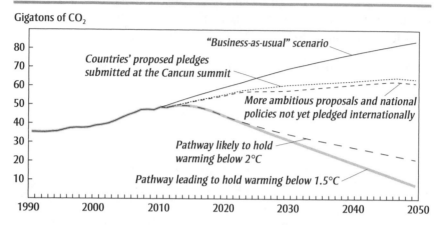

Source: Climate Action Tracker (climateactiontracker.com), © 2009 Ecofys and Climate Analytics.

The big problem with the pledges made by the major countries to cut emissions is that they are inadequate compared to what the scientific community says is necessary to keep climate change to manageable levels. As figure 1-1 shows, a group of MIT scientists who maintain an interactive real-time scoreboard calculate that even if all countries keep their pledges, the likely temperature rise by 2050 will be 3.2 degrees centigrade (5.8 degrees Fahrenheit). Although this would be better than the predicted temperature rise of 4.8 degrees centigrade (8.6 degrees Fahrenheit) under a "business-as-usual" scenario, it would still fall far short of the need to limit temperature rise to 2 degrees centigrade (3.6 degrees Fahrenheit) and emissions to below 450 ppm (parts per million). So, even on the most generous interpretation, the insurance policy against catastrophe was weak.

One year later, in Durban, the headline outcome was the agreement to start talks on a post-2020 climate accord. A new working group was given a mandate "to develop a protocol, another legal instrument or an agreed outcome with legal force under the United Nations Framework Convention on Climate Change (1992) applicable to all Parties." The job is to be completed by the end of 2015 to enable the agreement to go into effect and be implemented in 2020. The noteworthy and new part of this wording is that all countries are supposed to be legally bound, including the big developing-country emitters and the United States.[2]

Optimism has to be tempered by the fact that neither the magnitude nor the timing of commitments was specified, so it is not certain that the depressing emissions trajectory shown in figure 1-1 will be improved upon. Further clouding the outlook was the absence of details on the Green Climate Fund: who will contribute, how much, public funding or private, and if private, would it be via trade in emissions allocations?

Finally, the Rio+20 summit, held in June 2012, was never meant specifically to tackle or revive international cooperation on climate change. And it lived up to that expectation by producing a document of fifty-three pages of fine print described scathingly by a *New York Times* blogger as "283 paragraphs of kumbaya."[3] The final document contained some potentially useful ideas and promises. One was a commitment to devise new environmentally friendly development benchmarks in areas such as renewable energy and food security. It also gave a small boost to scrapping fossil fuel subsidies, but even here the draft agreement merely invited governments to "consider rationalising inefficient fossil fuel subsidies . . . in a manner that protects the poor and the affected communities."

## Why the Old Approach Won't Work

It is abundantly clear that the approach that has been used for climate change discussions over the past twenty years hasn't worked and won't work because of the three problems that we have labeled the "narrative" problem, the "adding-up" problem, and "new world" problem. We consider each in turn.

### The Narrative Problem

Climate change talks have not taken place in a historical vacuum. They have in fact been characterized by contentious and competing ethical and moral perspectives (discussed in detail in chapter 2). Developing countries look at recent history and argue that the rich world has been

2. Jan Von der Goltz, "Durban Climate Deal: What a Great Result This Would Have Been Some Ten Years Ago!" *Global Development: Views from the Center* (blog), December 13, 2011.

3. Mark McDonald, "U.N. Report from Rio on Environment a 'Suicide Note,'" *IHT Rendezvous* (blog), June 24, 2012.

responsible for the bulk of emissions and, having "colonized" emissions space, has preempted the growth and development prospects for developing countries. Relying on a broad ethical notion that all citizens of the world have equal access to the atmosphere's capacity as a carbon sink, they contend that their development opportunities should not be constrained.

Further, they are outraged that rich countries demand that they reduce their emissions, given that the difference in per capita energy use between rich and developing nations is so vast and that rich countries, especially the United States, have yet to seriously initiate the process of emissions reductions. They invoke the fact that U.S. emissions have actually increased since the 1997 Kyoto Protocol on emissions reductions (despite reductions since 2007) and find it galling that a nation of gas guzzlers, reluctant to give up its profligate ways, should be asking them to forgo the rudiments of modernity such as access to basic energy services. They also complain that rich countries have not shown enough generosity by way of financial and technology transfers to poor countries.

This narrative of recrimination has not gone unchallenged. At one extreme, Richard Cooper argues that "optimal decisions generally require [that] bygones . . . be ignored. To focus on equity, and thus the alleged retrospective wrongs of the remote past, is to assure inaction."[4] Vijay Joshi (2009), too, argues that the notion of historic responsibility is "a persuasive claim but it runs up against some powerful moral intuitions. The advanced countries did not expropriate knowingly. They acted in the belief, universally held until quite recently, that the atmosphere was an infinite resource. Moreover, the expropriators are mostly dead and gone. Their descendants, even if they could be identified, cannot be held responsible for actions they did not themselves commit."[5] For example, if only individuals can be responsible, then calculations from the Climate Analysis Indicator Tool (CAIT) suggest that just 8 percent of the 2000 emissions stock can be traced to the flow of emissions from individuals who are still alive and might be held responsible.[6]

---

4. Cooper (2008, p. 20).
5. Joshi (2009, pp. 130–31).
6. Posner and Weisbach (2010, table 5.1).

The rich countries have their own narrative of recalcitrance. They blame the major developing-country emitters such as China and India for not cooperating adequately and for being unwilling even to consider emissions cuts. Furthermore, claim some in the rich world, if we are responsible for pollution, then the developing world should be responsible for its large population. And if we are to be blamed for the "bads" such as emissions, then we should get credit for the "goods" that we have provided in the form of technology and research (such as those that led to the green revolution).

### The Adding-Up Problem

The adding-up problem is the brutal arithmetic that for the planet to survive in some habitable form, the world has to live within a fixed carbon budget of about 750 gigatons of $CO_2$ emissions between now and 2050. More allocations for one country mean less for another. The cold, hard fact is that a drastic reduction in aggregate emissions is required if we are to achieve a reasonable probability of keeping temperatures at livable levels. But the exercise is even more difficult than allocating a fixed carbon budget. Any attempt at allocation is a moving target because the carbon budget is actually shrinking relative to the growing needs of developing countries.

Until recently, the high-income countries, with one-sixth of the world's population, were responsible for the bulk of the greenhouse gases (GHGs) in the atmosphere. But China, India, and other developing-country emitters such as Brazil, Mexico, South Korea, Indonesia, South Africa, and Iran will progressively account for a larger share of total GHG emissions, meaning that without significant cuts from them, global targets cannot be met by actions by industrial countries alone.[7] In fact, the flows of $CO_2$ emissions by developing countries (the global South) have already exceeded those of the industrial countries (the global North). Even on a cumulative basis, developing-country emissions will exceed those of the industrial countries by around 2030.[8] Not much later, developing-country $CO_2$ emissions in a business-as-usual scenario (if no reductions are made and everyone continues on the current trajectory)

---

7. Joshi (2009).
8. Wheeler and Ummel (2007).

will greatly exceed the level of those consistent with keeping temperatures at reasonably safe levels (see figures 1-2a and 1-2b).

Moreover, given current rates of technological progress, the available carbon capacity is not even adequate to sustain business-as-usual growth rates for developing countries, let alone for the world as a whole (discussed in chapter 3). One striking calculation is that if the pace of technological change does not accelerate and if poorer countries preserve their development opportunities, rich countries will have to reduce their emissions by 270 percent! This means that they need to significantly *add* to the capacity of the atmosphere as a carbon sink—for example, by financing reforestation—for the overall carbon budget constraint to be met.

But could developing countries contribute to the atmosphere's carbon-sink capacity by cutting back emissions and ensuring safe global levels of $CO_2$? Unfortunately, emissions reductions for the foreseeable future would entail significant economic costs, given these countries' need for massive expansions in energy, transport, urban systems, and agricultural production for development. Current emissions are inequitably distributed across the world, with per capita emissions of developing countries a fraction of those of high-income countries (see figure 1-3). The implication is that any emissions cuts will reduce energy use and income even further beyond already low levels. Moreover, many of the large developing-country emitters are those with the better prospects for growing faster in the future, and emissions cuts would jeopardize these prospects. In short, given current technologies, growth and climate change goals are irreconcilable.[9]

Any commitments by developing countries to reduce emissions will lead to an increase in the price of energy and hence implicitly in the price of carbon, which is embodied in energy products. This price rise will affect not just the overall economy but also the composition of production and the distribution of consumption (see chapter 4). On the production side, manufacturing tends to be far more energy- and carbon-intensive than agriculture and services, so any increase in the carbon price is likely to lead to a contraction of manufacturing. In India, for example, the carbon intensity of manufacturing was about 518 tons per million U.S. dollars in 2004, much more than the 301 tons

9. Birdsall and others (2009).

FIGURE 1-2a. Poorer Country Emissions Are Overtaking Those of the Rich on an Annual Basis: Annual $CO_2$ Emissions, 1965–2035

Gigatons

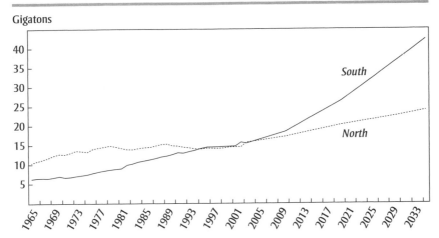

Source: Wheeler and Ummel (2007, p. 17).

FIGURE 1-2b. ...and Will Eventually Dominate Even on a Cumulative Basis: Cumulative $CO_2$ Emissions, 1965–2035

Gigatons

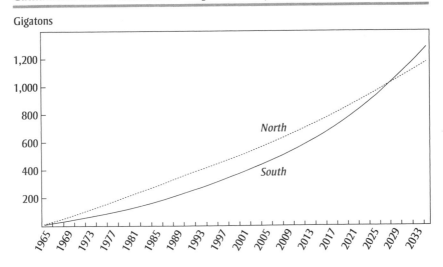

Source: Wheeler and Ummel (2007, p. 17).

**FIGURE 1-3.** **Richer Countries (to the right) Emit Far More per Capita Than Poorer Ones (to the left): International Distribution of Emissions, 2008**

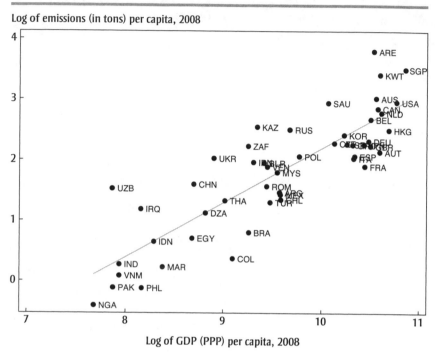

Source: Authors' calculations, based on data from the World Bank's World Development Indicators.

in agriculture and 231 tons in services. Of course, there are big differences within manufacturing, with certain energy-intensive manufacturing sectors emitting more than twice as much carbon as others.

In an international system of trading emissions rights, developing countries might have to cope with even higher carbon prices than if emission rights were not tradable. The reason is that if industrial countries undertake greater emissions cuts than developing countries and rights are not tradable, there will be international differences in carbon prices, with lower prices in developing countries than in industrial countries. But tradability—which is likely to involve producers in industrial countries' purchasing emission rights to discharge $CO_2$ in poorer countries— will lead to an international equalization of carbon prices, with prices in poorer countries rising by more than that entailed by their emissions cuts alone. Higher carbon prices could lead to the contraction of dynamic industries in developing countries, which would affect growth adversely.

The sales of emissions rights will lead to large capital flows into developing countries, and this can create the same types of complications as large aid flows or natural resource revenues. Unless the money can be effectively managed or prudently invested, the capital flows could lead to a contraction of the dynamic export sectors as the economy becomes uncompetitive through foreign exchange appreciation. For instance, we find that a plausible combination of carbon price increases and transfers generated through emissions trading could lead to a decline in India's manufacturing output by over 5 percent and in manufacturing exports by over 10 percent.

On the consumption side, higher carbon prices could hurt consumers of energy, including the very poor. The conventional view is that these distributional consequences can be addressed domestically through appropriate taxation and redistribution. But it is almost a condition of underdevelopment that politics and administrative capacity will impede such actions. The experience with industrial policies and "picking winners" has highlighted the demanding and often unfulfilled requirements for successfully doing so. Identifying and assisting the poor may be even harder, as dramatically illustrated in India, where the inability to target transfers has led to carbon-inefficient subsidies for power and kerosene that mostly benefit the non-poor.

Mahatma Gandhi may have been morally astute in lamenting that the planet can survive mankind's need but not his greed. But the adding-up problem suggests that given current technologies, even fairly meeting the reasonable needs of a growing world population will have dire planetary consequences. This problem can only be solved by shifting the focus away from emissions cuts to technology generation.

### The "New World" Problem

When the first major climate change talks took place, resulting in the 1997 Kyoto Protocol, there were, broadly, two sets of countries: large emitters that were, on average, rich, and medium to large emitters that were, on average, poor. Since then there have been significant shifts in economic power, and it is now estimated that nonindustrialized countries will account for 70 percent of world GDP by 2030 (measured in terms of purchasing power parity) and nearly 80 percent of incremental growth over the next twenty years.[10] China alone might account for 15 percent of world trade and 20 percent of GDP by 2030. And by then, China, India, and Brazil will rank among the five largest countries in the world in terms of their purchasing power parity.

Some of the most dramatic changes are likely to occur on the fiscal front. The public sector balance sheet of advanced economies has become extremely fragile, because of rising entitlements, aging populations, the global financial crises that began in 2008, and the contingent liabilities in their financial systems. The time bomb of fiscal unsustainability is ticking not just in the United States but also, perhaps even more furiously, in Europe. Whereas debt ratios for emerging-market Group of Twenty (G-20) countries are expected to remain steady at about 40 percent of GDP, those of advanced economies are expected to rise from close to 80 percent of GDP today to 120 percent by 2015 (see figure 1-4).[11] These ratios for industrial countries are not expected to reach reasonable levels until well into the future—if, that is, large fiscal adjustments are undertaken.

These numbers illustrate the obvious: the United States and Europe are no longer economically preeminent and must now deal with the new rising powers, including and especially China, India, Brazil, and Indonesia. These countries are large emitters—China is number 1 and India is number 3 in the emission rankings—and are now significant players in the world economic system and will have a significant say in the design of any international agreement. These new circumstances have implications for rich countries' being able to offer "carrots" such as financial transfers and wield "sticks," the threat of trade sanctions, as a way of inducing cooperative action.

Sticks-and-carrots tactics worked well in some situations. In the Uruguay Round of multilateral trade negotiations held between 1986 and 1994, which led to the establishment of the World Trade Organi-

10. Subramanian (2011). These projections assume relatively optimistic growth prospects for the United States and Europe.

11. These projections by the IMF are based on its assessment of current policies. In some ways, restricting the time horizon to 2015 understates U.S. and European fiscal problems. In the United States, the real challenges related to entitlements, especially health care, will emerge after 2020.

FIGURE 1-4. **Richest Countries Are Burdened with Debt: General Government Debt Ratios, 2000–14**

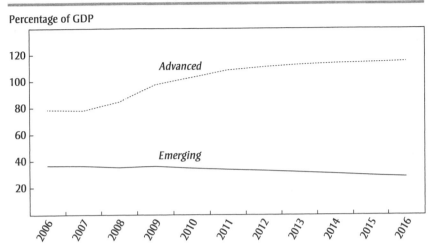

Percentage of GDP

Source: International Monetary Fund, "The State of Public Finances Cross-Country: Fiscal Monitor, November 2009" (Washington: IMF, November 3), p. 15 (www.imf.org/external/pubs/ft/spn/2009/spn0925.pdf).

zation (WTO), many developing countries were disinclined to change their intellectual property laws (IP). The United States and Europe threatened trade retaliation against a number of developing countries unless they changed their domestic IP laws. They also offered market access under bilateral free trade agreements, to Chile and Mexico, and multilaterally, in textiles and agricultural sectors (Subramanian 2011). That the use of sticks and carrots succeeded was reflected in the Agreement on Trade-Related Aspects of Intellectual Property Rights, which created new and substantially higher standards for IP protection around the world.

But a good example of the limits to carrots and sticks relates to China and its exchange rate policy: China keeps the value of the yuan low, which promotes higher exports. The United States wants China to revalue the yuan to a higher value vis-à-vis the U.S. dollar. Despite repeated U.S. cajoling and wielding of threats, China has not substantially changed its exchange rate, a policy that no doubt reflects its growing economic footprint, its huge market, and its pool of cash. In short, its international clout. If Niall Ferguson's famous term "Chimerica" to describe the intertwining of the United States and China means anything, it is that China has become so important and powerful a player that it is no longer easy to elicit cooperation from the outside.[12] Threats of trade and other sanctions are unlikely to work because China can retaliate—for example, by dumping its vast holdings of U.S. treasury paper—and cause disruption in Western markets.

In the context of climate change, the bargaining dynamic between the United States and large developing countries has been dominated by discussions of financial transfers to developing countries. How much money are we talking about? It is estimated that full compensation to developing countries for cutting current emissions by 30 percent would entail net financial transfers by the rich countries of about $430 billion in 2020, about 1.5 percent of their GDP, and about $3.3 trillion by 2050 (Jacoby and others 2008). Most of these flows would go to the four largest emitters. China and India would receive about $75 and $50 billion, respectively, in 2020 and about $600 billion and $175 billion, respectively, in 2050 (Jacoby and others 2008)—an event that is hard to imagine from a political point of view, especially given that in recent years China has in effect been writing checks to the U.S. government by financing its deficits.

If financial compensation in the form of public transfers from today's rich to poor is ruled out, what about private capital flows to developing countries? An article of faith in climate change discussions is that private resource flows to developing countries from the trading of emissions allocations can alleviate the costs to developing countries from emissions reductions (Stern 2009b). As the *Financial Times* editorialized, "In the actual world, a global scheme of tradable emissions quotas is the best solution" because trade in these quotas would automatically generate the transfers that could offset the costs imposed on developing countries.[13]

When all countries take on binding commitments to reduce emissions, capital flows will be generated through international trading of emissions allocations. How much countries gain is determined entirely by their emissions allocation. For large financial transfers to materialize, countries such as China and India would need to receive large allocations

---

12. Ferguson and Schularick (2007).

13. "We Cannot Gamble with the Planet," editorial, *Financial Times*, November 28, 2010.

of emissions rights. Yet the heart of the climate change divide is precisely that these large allocations to big developing countries are strongly resisted by rich countries. There may be a kind of "transfer illusion" based on the notion that it is harder to make public financial transfers than generous allocations of emissions rights—after all, it is this illusion that favors cap-and-trade over taxes in a domestic context. But it seems unlikely that this transfer illusion or obfuscation can overcome the fundamental economic and political realities that transfers will be large and hence economically unaffordable; and the potential recipients of transfers or emissions allocations will be the economically dynamic countries China and India.

## Cooperation in the New World

Any prospect for success going forward will need to address each of the three problems we have identified.

### A New Narrative

Narratives matter. Not just for creating and sustaining nationhood, as Isaiah Berlin famously argued, but also, critically, in international negotiations. In the climate change talks, the old narrative must give way to a new one. In our view, the key shift will have to come from the DEEs, with China, India, Brazil, and Indonesia proactively leading the charge for action on climate change. But is this credible or plausible? We believe it is, for two reasons.

First, it is increasingly recognized that the stakes in the near to medium term are much greater for the developing countries than for today's rich countries. They are either in or much closer to the tropics, where rising average temperatures will more quickly reduce agricultural productivity. They have much higher population densities, and therefore much narrower margins for survival as natural systems, especially water, come under stress. And they have much lower per capita incomes, making it harder to cope with coming disruptions by making major infrastructure investments such as building sea walls or extending irrigation systems.

William R. Cline (2007) estimates the costs for agriculture. In the event of a 2.5 percent temperature increase, India's long-term agricultural productivity will decline by about 38 percent, as compared with a U.S.

decline of 6 percent. Overall, India and sub-Saharan Africa will suffer losses of as much as 4 to 5 percent of their GDP from a 2.5 percent temperature increase, compared with less than 0.5 percent of GDP for the United States and Japan.

More recently, William Nordhaus (2011) has calculated the social cost of carbon in terms of the change in long-run consumption due to an additional unit of emissions. He estimates that this social cost is significantly greater for China, India, and other developing countries than it is for the United States or Europe. For example, the social cost of carbon for China is about three times that of the United States and nearly four times that of Europe. For India it is about two times that of the United States and three times that of Europe. These greater costs for China and India result from these countries' greater growth prospects, which would be negatively affected by climate change, and their greater vulnerability to damage from climate change.

Indeed, the alarming prospect for the DEEs is not that they will be asked to contribute too much but that the rich countries might ask too little. The rich countries, reluctant to cut emissions, may opt to interpret inaction by the DEEs as justification for attempting to adapt to climate change instead of taking aggressive actions to avert it. If the rich make this strategic choice, the consequence could be catastrophic for all parties. As the writer Simon Kuper put it, "We in the West have recently made an unspoken bet: we're going to wing it, run the risk of climate catastrophe, and hope that it is mostly faraway people in poor countries who will suffer."[14] The large and vulnerable developing countries must go on a war footing to campaign for action, including by today's rich countries, to avert catastrophic climate change.

A second reason why DEEs will be obliged to take the lead is because industrialized countries are increasingly incapable of doing so. The political consensus for serious action is fraying, especially in the United States. Regarding President Barack Obama's position, the political columnist Hendrik Hertzberg noted that there is a gulf between candidate Obama's passionate embrace of climate change as humanity's and his top concern and President Obama's token allusion to climate

14. Simon Kuper, "Climate Change: Who Cares Anymore?" *FT.com*, September 17, 2011.

change in his 2011 State of the Union address, in the context of energy efficiency.[15] One explanation for Obama's inaction may be the combination of economic problems—high unemployment, low growth, and diminishing prospects for the middle class—that increasingly preoccupy American policymakers. No doubt this tension between the economy and the environment is reflected in the administration's ambivalence toward the Keystone XL oil pipeline from Canada to the Gulf of Mexico. Then, too, the U.S. political and intellectual environment—characterized by the rise of those who don't accept the science of climate change and the rise of the fuel-funded lobby actively opposed to action on climate change—offers little encouragement.

In the past, the DEEs, especially China and India, were accused of being recalcitrants because they were apparently unwilling to assume their "fair" share of the responsibility for climate change action. Now, the growing political acceptance in these countries of the need to act on climate change is creating a serious possibility of a role reversal. But for China and India to articulate the new narrative, to credibly become the new *demandeurs,* they must back up their rhetoric with real contributions to the long-term solution.

### A New Arithmetic

If large transfers are off the table, developing countries can meet climate change goals without sacrificing their economic dynamism if they spew less $CO_2$ for the same amount of activity. This is only possible through rapid technological change—indeed, through radical, historically unprecedented technological breakthroughs.

How radical would this breakthrough have to be? In chapter 3 we discuss the magnitude of technology improvement and energy conservation needed to ensure that climate change objectives are met without developing countries' having to sacrifice their growth and energy-use goals. Changes of the required magnitude in consumers' energy use and producers' efficiency in the use of carbon were not observed even after the oil shocks of the 1970s, which led to an increase in the price of energy far greater than that contemplated under any of the current proposals on

---

15. Henrik Hertzberg, "Cooling on Warming," *The New Yorker,* February 7, 2011.

emissions mitigations. At that time, efficiency in the use of carbon increased only by about one-third of what it will take in the future to meet climate change goals.

### A New World Focus

But how can countries cooperate to generate the required technological progress? The key will be for the industrial countries to recognize that premature cuts in carbon emissions by developing countries would threaten these countries' economic dynamism. At the same time, the DEEs must focus on what they need to contribute, consistent with their new dynamism, to get the industrialized countries to undertake ambitious emissions cuts. Rather than seeing these emissions cuts as payback for historic sins, they should view these cuts as an investment to help all parties in generating technology, thereby helping to reduce the future cost of their own emissions cuts.

The framing of the issue, at least in the ongoing dialogue, would shift from "cash from industrial countries for cuts by developing countries" to "contributions from developing countries for cuts by industrial countries." Such a change in substance and attitude by developing countries could set in motion a mutually reinforcing dynamic of cooperation. Thus, the formula, informed fully by basic notions of equity, would be "To developing countries according to their growth needs; from developing countries commensurate with their economic dynamism, and to all the common good of planetary survival." This would be the basis for a "Greenprint" for international cooperation.

## The Logic of the "Greenprint"

What does our proposed Greenprint look like? The new approach will not look like the old one. The contrast between the old and new approaches is one of moving from a backward-looking narrative—the rich are to blame—to a forward-looking one—the emerging markets will suffer more and hence these countries must take the lead (see box 1-1). The changed narrative enables a new focus, approach, and set of actions that lead to different results. Here it should be noted that the set of actions that we are proposing for the two major groups of economies, today's rich industrial economies and the dynamic emerging ones, should be seen as one possible selection from among a broad menu

**BOX 1-1.** Contrast between Old Approach and "Greenprint for Cooperation"

| OLD APPROACH | NEW "GREENPRINT FOR COOPERATION" APPROACH |
|---|---|
| **Narrative** | |
| *Backward-looking*—Industrial countries are to blame. | *Forward-looking*—Emerging-market countries are more vulnerable to consequences of climate change and thus must take the lead. |
| **Focus** | |
| *On emissions cuts*, because required cuts are considered attainable at acceptable cost. | *On technological progress*, because required emissions cuts are not attainable at acceptable cost with current technologies (the "adding-up" problem). |
| **Distribution of burden** | |
| *Industrial countries* must bear nearly all costs. | *All countries* must contribute to a solution, consistent with their economic situation. |
| **Actions** | |
| Industrial countries and emerging-market countries both cut emissions. Industrial countries compensate emerging-market countries for losses caused by the latters' emissions cuts. | Industrial countries make early emissions cuts. Emerging-market countries: <br>• contribute to fund for developing and disseminating new technologies <br>• commit to making future cuts, conditional on development of new technologies <br>• allow industrial countries to take trade actions under WTO auspices against imports from emerging markets where comparable emissions cuts have not been implemented |
| **Results** | |
| Aggregate emissions cuts consistent with climate change goals. | Aggregate emissions cuts consistent with climate change goals but attained at lower developmental cost because of technological progress. |

Source: Authors.

of options. Our aim is to highlight that any plausible plan for cooperation would have to be vastly different from the current one.[16]

Central to our proposal is providing incentives to generate technology that addresses the adding-up problem and to calibrate contributions to current economic conditions. To this end, we propose the following two suites of actions:

—The rich countries would commit to an early and sustained increase in the price of carbon, targeting a steady-state price of carbon consistent with creating a path of emissions reductions that would bring emissions per capita down from just about twenty tons now to two tons in all industrialized countries by 2050—in keeping with a 80 percent reduction from 2005 levels.[17] This carbon price would be the key price signal to galvanize the green technology revolution.

—The large developing countries would complement and facilitate this industrial-country action in a number of key ways: contribute to a global fund for green technology development; allow, under special conditions, industrial countries to impose limited carbon-based border taxes; and commit to future emissions cuts, conditional on improvements in technology; and they would not raise the price of carbon.

DEEs' not raising the price of carbon could create a competitiveness problem for industrial-country producers and hence a political problem for industrial-country governments seeking to raise the price of carbon in the first place. By agreeing to border taxes on carbon, DEEs would be helping industrial-country governments address their domestic political economy problem. If DEEs were able to take the types of actions mentioned, they could comfortably claim the mantle of leadership on climate change, thereby altering the narrative.

If all parties implemented these actions, we would expect green technological change to be galvanized and better technologies to start flowing. At that stage, it would become easier for the DEEs to take on emissions reductions obligations, which would be triggered when certain

16. It is an open question as to whether cooperation should follow the current paradigm of seeking one grand agreement or involve a variety of loosely coordinated smaller-scale agreements (Barrett and Toman 2010).

17. The carbon price that can achieve the emissions reductions objective will of course be intensely debated because it will depend on a host of economic, technological, and ethical factors.

technology thresholds are met, such as the price of renewables falling sufficiently relative to fossil fuels. Specifying these thresholds, and calibrating individual countries' emissions obligations to these thresholds and other economic circumstances, would need to be carefully discussed and perhaps would need to be enshrined in legal commitments.

## A Menu of Options for DEE Contributions

In this section we elaborate on the specific contributions that DEEs could choose to take.

1. From receiving to forgoing to giving: an emerging-market Green Technology Fund
2. Accommodating modest border taxes to facilitate deeper emissions cuts by industrial countries
3. Technology triggers: conditionally committing to cut future emissions
4. Committing to phase out fossil fuel subsidies
5. New carrots with sticks

These contributions would be in lieu of their own cuts and a quid pro quo for significant emissions cuts by industrial countries. Not all developing countries would be expected to make contributions—only those whose economic dynamism has enabled them to attain a certain development threshold, and contributions would be calibrated to relative economic strength. The threshold would be more or less defined by the countries in the IMF's emerging economies group. Countries below this threshold would be exempt and remain net recipients of finance and technology. Contributions could come from both what countries actually do (such as providing finance and technology) and what they forgo (the right to seek compensation, to acquire technology at less than market cost, and to preserve existing access to foreign markets).

### 1. From Receiving to Forgoing to Giving: An Emerging Market Green Technology Fund

Large developing countries continue to see themselves as potential recipients of financial inflows. The new reality, however, is that industrial countries simply cannot afford to provide financial compensation for action on climate change. DEEs could make a virtue of this new reality. One option would be simply to declare, as China has implicitly done, that they would not be claimants for international transfers related to climate change. A more ambitious option would be to help set up and even contribute to an international fund for technology generation and dissemination.

The good news is that if industrial countries undertake ambitious emissions cuts, technology generation will be given a sharp boost. But the problem for developing countries is that much of this technology might be created in the private sector, underpinned by strong intellectual property (IP) protection. Developing countries can seek access to this technology by demanding that IP regimes be weakened, as they have demanded in the past. But this could weaken the incentive to create the right technologies in industrial countries as well as in their own markets, which are large and growing. In the event that new green technologies are not easily copied, weak IP regimes become a disincentive for technology transfer. In this case, the international fund could finance the technology transfer.

Such a fund could have a second objective: to provide incentives for creating a public "commons" of green technologies, with the clear understanding that any such technologies would be freely available because they would not have been privately funded. This part of the fund could be set up as advance market commitments, financial commitments to subsidize future purchases of a product or service up to predetermined prices and volumes. Michael Kremer and Rachel Glennerster (2004) have shown how such a structure could be applied to developing a pneumococcal vaccine in a pilot project by the GAVI Alliance and the World Bank (see also Berndt and others 2007). A coordinated technology fund could overcome problems of fragmentation and insufficient incentives that might arise from purely national efforts.

This new fund could be the first postwar and post–G-20 international institution with a governance structure reflecting the economic importance of large developing countries. Contributions could be based on two criteria, ability to pay and potential benefits, which would differentiate these countries on a simple, fair, and transparent basis. If twenty-two emerging market countries contributed about 0.2 percent of their GDP annually over fifteen years, their contribution alone to the global technology fund would be about half a trillion dollars.

## 2. Accommodating Modest Border Taxes to Facilitate Deeper Emissions Cuts by Industrial Countries

One possible impediment to ambitious emissions cuts by rich countries when they are not being made by developing countries is that the rich countries' energy-intensive producers would be at a competitive disadvantage if the price of carbon were higher for them than for others. In fact, we estimate that with even modest emissions mitigation actions by the United States, its energy-intensive, internationally exposed firms would experience export and output declines of 12 percent and 4 percent, respectively (discussed in chapter 5).

How can these competitiveness concerns be addressed? One way is through legislation now in draft form in the United States and the European Union to provide free allowances to vulnerable producers, those in trade-intensive and energy-intensive sectors. These allowances, which are essentially political pork, would be costly in fiscal terms, but they would soften the resistance to climate change action and head off the clamor from domestic industry groups for trade actions.

We believe, however, that the current fiscal problems in the rich countries have so altered circumstances that free emissions allowances will seem less attractive politically than border taxes as a way of meeting competitiveness concerns. Recently, Senators John Kerry of Massachusetts and Lindsey Graham of South Carolina stated: "There is no reason we should surrender our marketplace to countries that do not accept environmental standards. For this reason, we should consider a border tax on items produced in countries that avoid these standards. This is consistent with our obligations under the World Trade Organization." Nicolas Sarkozy has stated: "We need to impose a carbon tax at [Europe's] borders. I will lead that battle." At the same time, there is a growing intellectual legitimization for these taxes. The Nobel Prize–winning economist Paul Krugman—generally a proponent of free trade—has issued his own endorsement of carbon taxes at the border, arguing that they are "a matter of leveling the playing field, not protectionism."[18]

18. John Kerry and Lindsey Graham, "Yes We Can (Pass Climate Change Legislation)," op-ed, *New York Times,* October 10, 2009; Sarkozy quoted in Peggy Hollinger, "Sarkozy Calls for Carbon Tax on Imports," *FT.com,* September 10, 2009; Paul Krugman, "Climate, Trade, Obama," *The Conscience of a Liberal* (blog), June 29, 2009.

If the DEEs agreed to border taxes on carbon being imposed by rich-country governments, it would help the latter deal with their domestic political economy problem. At the same time, the DEEs could explicitly formalize the prohibition of more extreme forms of trade action. For the United States and the EU, the possibility of trade actions could reassure domestic energy-intensive industries and environmentalists that they would not be "surrendering the marketplace" or exporting carbon to countries with lower environmental standards.

The question is whether such taxes can be designed in a way that addresses industrial countries' concerns regarding competitiveness while limiting the trade costs for developing countries. What has to be avoided is the imposition of tariffs applied across-the-board on the basis of the carbon content of imports, which would be a "nuclear option" in terms of trade consequences. For example, such an action by the United States and the EU would be the equivalent of imposing a tariff of over 20 percent on China and India, resulting in lost exports of about 20 percent.

We see two possible solutions. One would be across-the-board tariffs and rebates for exporters based on the carbon content *in domestic production*. These would almost completely offset the adverse effects on U.S. output and exports of energy-intensive manufactures, while limiting declines in China's and India's manufacturing exports to about 2 percent.

Another possibility would be tariffs based on the carbon content of imports but applied only to a narrow set of carbon-intensive products. These would dampen the adverse effect of emissions reductions on U.S. output and exports of energy-intensive manufactures, which would decline by only about 0.5 percent and 7 percent, respectively, while limiting declines in China's and India's manufacturing exports to about 3 percent. But this option would be tougher to implement because it would require information on foreign countries' carbon content and hence would be more prone to abuse by protectionists.

### 3. Technology Triggers: Conditionally Committing to Cut Future Emissions

Lord Nicholas Stern has argued that developing countries should "conditionally commit to commit." By this he means that the key conditions for them to cut their emissions would be ambitious emissions reductions by the industrial countries and the delivery of financial assistance. Ambitious emissions reductions by industrialized nations would still be a key condition because that is the sine qua non for incentivizing technological progress. However, the Stern condition on financial assistance is now politically infeasible, at least for India and China, as discussed earlier.

The reason for developing countries to commit to some emissions reductions is to strengthen the incentives for technology creation in the long run by assuring innovators of a bigger market that would include the large developing countries. But this commitment is only credible if technological progress mitigates the costs to developing countries of emissions reductions.

Accordingly, developing country emissions reductions could be made conditional on, or triggered by, technology improvements in key areas such as carbon capture and storage; car battery; fuel efficiency, and so forth (Patel 2010). Future discussions should establish how these technology triggers could work in practice. This approach is consistent with developing countries' willingness, expressed at Durban, to take on legally binding commitments in the future.

### 4. Committing to Phase Out Fossil Fuel Subsidies

Developing countries could directly contribute to climate change mitigation by committing to phase out subsidies for fossil fuel consumption, which impose large economic costs within these countries, especially because they encourage profligacy in the use of water for agriculture. These water-related costs will only increase in the presence of climate change and growing water scarcity. Of course, there could even be a quid pro quo, with the DEEs demanding a reciprocal elimination of tax breaks for the fossil fuel industry in rich countries.

The OECD estimates that the removal of energy subsidies in all non-OECD countries would lead to a substantial decline in emissions from fossil fuel consumption, amounting to a 10 percent decline in global GHG emissions in 2050 compared to business-as-usual. China's emissions would be reduced by over 10 percent, India's by close to 25 percent, and Russia's and other oil-exporting countries' by around 30 percent.

### 5. New Carrots and Sticks

Note that in the old approach, the rich countries were wielding the carrots of financial transfers to induce emissions cuts by the poor countries and the stick of trade action as the penalty for not undertaking such cuts.

In the Greenprint we envisage some significant role reversal as to who brandishes the sticks and who offers the carrots, reflecting shifts in economic weight and power. The DEEs would implicitly be offering carrots if, consistent with their fiscal strength, they were to make financial contributions to the Green Technology Fund that would benefit all countries, and if, to facilitate emissions cuts, they were to allow rich countries to take trade actions against the exports of DEEs.

Could the DEEs also wield sticks against any failure of the rich to contribute to climate change prevention? One possibility would be for the DEEs to threaten to take trade action against the exports of rich countries—or at least their energy-intensive exports—if they failed to undertake the early emissions cuts that, according to the Greenprint, are critical to unleash technological innovation.

The DEEs could even enact legislation according to which they could take trade-restrictive action against all countries that exceeded a target level of per capita emissions (say, five tons) by 2025. Such a stick would be a natural complement to the carrot of constructive engagement that they would offer. The stick would also implicitly help set an international standard of equity and fairness on emissions targets that is an alternative to the current one, advanced by industrial countries, of reductions in absolute emissions.

Such a dramatic role reversal could play a part in breaking the policy paralysis on climate change in the rich countries, especially the United States. If, for example, the DEEs target U.S. manufacturing exports, these industries could be galvanized into putting pressure on the carbon-based sectors to loosen their grip on climate change policy.

For a dramatic role reversal whereby the DEEs wield sticks against the rich for noncooperation to have credibility, it might be necessary for the DEEs to either take or commit to some serious actions that put serious pressure on rich countries. One possibility might be for the DEEs to eliminate fossil fuel subsidies, or to commit to achieving that goal within, say, five years, and set a path for future carbon prices. They could then more credibly threaten trade action if the rich countries do not undertake emissions cuts.

## Is the New Approach Plausible?

What are the odds that our proposed Greenprint would be embraced by either the large developing-country emitters or the rich countries, especially the United States?

There is reason for optimism regarding the large developing-country emitters because they are already following the same approach domestically. To preserve its existing comparative advantage, China is not confronting traditional manufacturers with higher carbon prices. Instead, it is providing incentives for green technologies to help its comparative advantage evolve in new directions. It plans to generate 15 percent of its energy from renewable sources by 2020. In 2007 China invested $12 billion in renewable energy, which placed it second in the world in absolute dollars spent, just behind Germany. Over the next decade it plans to spend between $440 billion and $660 billion on new energy development, made doable by its economic dynamism and strong fiscal picture.

India and other large developing-country emitters such as South Africa are acting similarly: instead of raising the price of carbon, they are paying much higher prices for renewable energy sources. India has begun reducing fuel subsidies and deregulating the pricing of some petroleum products; it intends to generate 15 percent of its total power from renewable sources by 2020. David Wheeler and Saurabh Shome (2009) estimate that this policy is equivalent to a total $CO_2$ charge of about $80 billion for emissions from new coal-fired power facilities between 2010 and 2020. The relative price changes induced in this manner may have a less disruptive effect on downstream users of energy than an increase in carbon prices, with the government absorbing the dislocation costs that would otherwise be imposed on the private sector.

More broadly, this strategy is resulting in large developing countries' taking the lead in shifting to low-carbon energy development. For example, Wheeler (2010) estimates that 68 percent of the increase in low-carbon energy generation—including biomass, solar, wind, geothermal, hydro, and nuclear—during the period from 2002 to 2008 has been in developing countries.

Are we asking too much of developing countries? We don't think so. First, our approach reflects the key equity principle of preserving full development opportunities for the poorer countries; that is why they would not be required to make any significant emissions cuts initially. Second, consistent with this equity principle, it is industrialized countries that would be required to make ambitious (large in magnitude and front-loaded) emissions cuts. Third, many of the contributions we suggest merely internationalize actions that the DEEs are already pursuing domestically. Fourth, our proposed contributions are a menu of options rather than a must-do package.

As for rich countries, amid the generally gloomy political climate, there may be some spurs for action. Just as the melting of the Himalayan glaciers has aroused a new sense of urgency in India, so the repeated forest fires in the western United States, coinciding with nine of the ten hottest years ever recorded, can shake the United States out of its torpor.[19]

Second, the United States faces a medium-term fiscal crisis of unprecedented proportions. The arithmetic is such that new sources of revenue will have to be found to bridge the deficit, and taxes on carbon or the auctioning of any carbon caps could feature prominently as part of the solution to the fiscal crisis. Action on climate change could thus be forced by fiscal rather than scientific or moral imperatives. In 2011 Professor Alan Blinder made a case for a U.S. carbon tax of 8 cents on every gallon of gasoline in 2013, rising to 26 cents by 2015, to kick in after the current recovery takes hold.[20] He argues that such a tax not only would address the U.S. fiscal problem but also would be good for the environment, stimulate innovation in green technologies, and reduce fuel dependence.

Third, the shale gas revolution has made available a cleaner source of energy, which will make it easier for the United States to meet given emission targets. Put differently, the carbon tax that will need to be imposed by the United States will likely be lower than previously, even though some of the emission benefits may be diluted because of the reduced incentives to develop even cleaner sources of energy such as solar and wind.

In addition, the United States might be motivated by a desire to avoid a trade conflict with Europe, which notwithstanding its ongoing

19. The implications for emissions reductions of the Fukushima tragedy in Japan remain unclear. Germany, for example, announced a policy to phase out nuclear power plants. Whether such reactions signal just a shift away from nuclear energy or a renewed interest in other sources with a clear impetus toward reduced GHG emissions remains to be seen.

20. Alan S. Blinder, "The Carbon Tax Miracle Cure," *Wall Street Journal,* January 31, 2011.

economic difficulties has a durable interest in climate change policy. If Europe takes further action on this front, it will want to safeguard the competitiveness of its energy-intensive industries from those not similarly encumbered by carbon taxes. In air transport, the EU is already insisting that foreign airlines operating in Europe buy emissions quotas just as European airlines will be obliged to do. The irony is that the United States, which has considered wielding the trade instrument against recalcitrant developing countries, might find itself the target of such instruments.

Then, too, the United States might be roused into action by the growing technological threat from China. Already, U.S. business has been alarmed at China's attempts to develop technology in other areas through government support and obtaining technologies from abroad. The thought that China could easily replicate these actions in the new green areas is weighing heavily on U.S. business and government.

## Conclusion

Reducing greenhouse gas emissions to prevent catastrophic climate change needs a new Greenprint for international cooperation. The pre-Copenhagen formula of "cash for cuts" was predicated on a division of the world into rich and poor. The recent financial crisis and the longer-term forces of economic convergence have combined to put that world behind us. Now, an economically enfeebled industrial world must engage with a financially strong and economically confident developing world on the basis of a new assessment of strengths and constraints.

Will cooperation on climate change be easy? Almost certainly not. But we are confident that the current approach will not work. That is why in writing this book we have attempted to provide ammunition to escape the stranglehold of the old approach, characterized by a narrative of recrimination and recalcitrance. Developing countries focus on the past, when rich countries "colonized" the carbon space, and seek contributions commensurate with historic responsibility. In contrast, industrial countries focus on the hypothetical future, when the dynamic developing countries will be large emitters, and complain that the future despoilers are unwilling to begin making contributions now.

We urgently need a new narrative, one characterized by leadership and innovation. In particular, developing countries must recognize their immense stakes in averting climate change, stakes that are even greater than those for the rich world, which will be affected less and has more resources to adapt. They must now take the lead and prod an increasingly reluctant West, especially the United States, to act. By making meaningful contributions of their own, they can claim the mantle of leadership. This means bringing into play policy instruments beyond carbon pricing, redefining the categories of rich and poor, and modifying the roles of financiers and recipients of funds. Our Greenprint suggests a way to help efface humanity's potentially catastrophic carbon footprint.

# Equity in Climate Change:
# An Analytical Review

... and the awareness
of things ill done and done to others' harm
which once you took for exercise of virtue.
—T. S. Eliot, *Four Quartets,* "Little Gidding"

In some fundamental sense, the equity debate in the context of climate change has been an attempt on the part of developing countries to create or instill an "awareness" in industrial economies of the "harm" they are believed to have caused during their remarkable economic and industrial progress, beginning with the Industrial Revolution in the late 1700s. Of course, the harm to others from carbon-based progress was largely, and until recently, an unintended consequence of virtuous industrialization (called "collateral damage" by some). But instilling this awareness of past harmful actions and their current effects is nevertheless felt to be critical to generating the right "narrative" so that climate change negotiations going forward can produce equitable outcomes that all countries can live with and hence abide by.

But what is the harm? Should we move beyond notions of "harm"? How should one think more broadly about equity, and about achieving it? This chapter provides an analytical structure to bring together the existing attempts to answer these questions. The literature on equity in climate change is voluminous. In this chapter we do not attempt to cover all the contributions that have been made on equity and climate change but focus on the more important and more recent ones.

## FIGURE 2-1. International Distribution of Emissions, 2008

Log of emissions (in tons) per capita, 2008

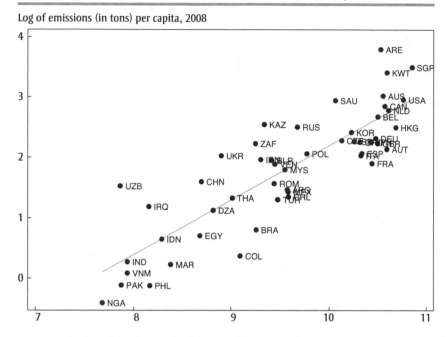

Source: Authors' calculations based on data from the World Bank's World Development Indicators.

At the outset, it is worth asking why equity has acquired such salience in the context of climate change. Figures 2-1 and 2-2 suggest a reason. Figure 2-1 plots per capita $CO_2$ emissions against GDP per capita (PPP) for a sample of fifty countries for 2008, the latest year for which data are available. The figure shows a positive and statistically significant relationship between these two variables: richer countries have substantially greater per capita emissions. Figure 2-2 provides data on per capita energy use, for household energy and road travel, for some of the major industrial and developing countries. That many of the developing countries consume a fraction of the energy consumed in the rich world suggests that many energy needs remain unmet: for example, the average Indian's energy consumption is 5 percent of U.S. levels. That the current distribution of emissions and energy use across the world is highly inequitable is widely recognized.

**FIGURE 2-2.** Per Capita Energy Use (Households and Transportation) as Percentage of U.S. Use, 2005

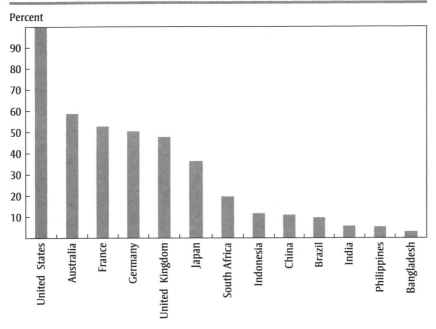

Source: World Bank's World Development Indicators.

How equity considerations should inform future action on climate change is less clear.

## Equity Principles for Allocating Emissions

Central to our analysis are the principles for determining emissions allocations, the amount of carbon dioxide each country should be "allowed" to emit. Equity can be based on certain inherent notions of fairness, including concepts of rights, regardless of their consequences. Equity can also be evaluated in terms of the consequences of different emissions allocations, and typically these consequences relate to economic outcomes or the economic welfare of individuals and nations. The former is the deontological approach (concerned with duties and rights) while the latter is referred to as the consequentialist, or welfarist, approach, the view that the value of an action derives solely from the value of its consequences (Posner and Weisbach, 2010; Dietz, Hepburn, and Stern 2007).[1]

Our reading of the literature suggests that four principles for the equitable allocations of emissions recur, encompassing both fairness-based or intrinsic criteria as well as consequentialist criteria. We also consider another criterion based on adjustment costs. (See appendix table 2-1 for a list of papers in the equity literature and the equity principle or principles their authors advocate.)

## 1. Equal per Capita Emissions

The first fairness-based criterion is that regardless of past actions and future opportunities, every citizen of the planet today has an equal right to the atmosphere as a reservoir for absorbing greenhouse gas emissions. This criterion is rooted in the idea that all humans are created equal, and this includes from the perspective of enjoying the environmental services of the atmosphere. This has become widely known as the per capita approach because it implies that per capita emissions would be the same across countries.

This principle has been emphasized over the years by a number of developing countries, going back to A. Agarwal and S. Narain (1991), Dubash (2009a), Saran (2009), and Ghosh (2010). More recently, in the context of carbon budgeting, too, the equal per capita principle is being reemphasized by the German Advisory Council on Climate Change (2009) as well as by Kanitkar and others (2010). Even some who do not give exclusive status to the equal per capita principle—such as Bosetti and Frankel (2009) and Parikh and Parikh (2009)—do consider it relevant in any discussion of equity.

Posner and Weisbach (2010), and Posner and Sunstein (2008) contend that the equal per capita principle is superficially appealing but in practice is an inefficient way of attaining equity or redressing inequity

---

1. A point on terminology: In the literature and in this chapter, the terms "emissions allocations" and "emissions rights" are used interchangeably. But it should be noted that the conceptual basis of the term "emissions rights" is not uncontroversial (see below). Even if we use the term "emissions rights," we do not intend it to connote an ethical right to pollution.

because population and incomes are not negatively correlated: that is, giving greater emissions allocations to countries with large populations would not necessarily be the same as giving greater allocations to poor countries. A stark example would be to take two countries that are broadly similar in population: the United States and Indonesia. The equal per capita principle would allocate similar emissions to both countries, but that would not be equitable because the average Indonesian is much poorer than the average American and hence deserving of more rights to energy use that would entail greater emissions. Frankel (2007) implicitly supports the equal per capita principle as the target that all countries would attain in the very long run as their incomes converge.

Although the targets proposed by Stern (2009c) would lead to equal per capita emissions by 2050, Stern (2009b) is ambivalent about the ethical basis of the equal per capita principle when it comes to allocations. This ambivalence is based in part on the view that although there can be rights to "goods," for example, the environmental services of the atmosphere, there is no symmetric right to "bads," such as the right to pollute the global commons. It is also based in part on the view that broad ethical claims such as rights to development or participation are more defensible than claims to a narrower set of goods and services.

## 2. Historic Responsibility

A second and perhaps more controversial fairness-based criterion relates future rights to liabilities for past emissions. This notion is based on the fact that the threat of climate change stems from the limited capacity of the atmosphere to absorb certain greenhouse gases. Thus, the atmosphere can be likened to a reservoir. The more greenhouse gases have been spewed into the atmosphere, the more it fills up and the less space there is left for subsequent emissions of gases. The historic-responsibility principle suggests that the allocation of future emissions should be inversely related to a country's past emissions. The historic-responsibility principle is based on the ethical notion that "thou shalt not harm others" or at least not harm others "knowingly" and that if harm is done there should be compensation. In effect, this is like the polluter-pays principle: past polluters "pay" by having a lesser claim to future emissions (World Bank 2009).

This historic-responsibility principle also has a long and illustrious pedigree in climate change negotiations. Among those who have invoked this principle are Stern (2009b), Winkler, Brouns, and Kartha (2006), German Agency for Technical Cooperation (2004), Müller and others (2007), Winkler (2010), Bhagwati (2009a, 2009b), Kanitkar and others (2010), Pan and others (2008), Panagariya (2009), Parikh and Parikh (2009), and Dubash (2009b). It is discussed also in Posner and Sunstein (2008), Posner and Weisbach (2010), Cooper (2008), and Joshi and Patel (2009). One of the first contributions to actually elaborate on and quantify the notion of historic responsibility was the proposal made by Brazil to the United Nations Framework Convention on Climate Change meetings in 1997 (Government of Brazil 1997).

But the notion of historic responsibility has been challenged, and the exact way this principle could be translated into policy has also been controversial. An extreme position on historic responsibility is Cooper (2008), who argues that "optimal decisions generally require bygones to be ignored. To focus on equity, and thus the alleged retrospective wrongs of the remote past, is to assure inaction" (p. 20).

Posner and Weisbach (2010) argue that a retributive justice perspective on historic responsibility normally requires establishing an injurer who behaved in a "morally culpable" way and establishing the identity of the injured or the victim. In the climate change context, this argument leads to the question of whether the perpetrator is an individual or a country. If only individuals can bear responsibility, then according to calculations from the Climate Analysis Indicator Tool (CAIT), only 8 percent of the stock of emissions in 2000 can be traced to the flow of emissions from individuals who are still alive and might be held responsible for those emissions (Posner and Weisbach 2010, table 5.1).

Joshi (2009) argues that the notion of historic responsibility is "a persuasive claim but it runs up against some powerful moral intuitions. The advanced countries did not expropriate knowingly. They acted in the belief, universally held until quite recently, that the atmosphere was an infinite resource. Moreover, the expropriators are mostly dead and gone. Their descendants, even if they could be identified, cannot be held responsible for actions they did not themselves commit" (pp. 130–31).

Bhagwati (2009b) argues that reparations for past harm can be imposed on countries and invokes precedents in U.S. law. He distinguishes between stocks of emissions (the cumulative emissions over the last several hundred years) and future flows of emissions, arguing that countries should pay for past damage. Although he does not argue that past responsibility should determine future emissions allocations per se (which in his view should be determined separately), he nevertheless argues that rich nations should pay compensation for the damage they have caused by their past emissions. There is a precedent of such a fund in the U.S. legal system: the Comprehensive Environmental Response, Compensation, and Liability Act (CERCLA), passed in 1980, commonly known as the "Superfund," under which a tax is levied on polluting industries and liability is established for the release of hazardous waste at closed and abandoned waste sites.

Philosophers are still debating whether corrective justice requires establishment of culpability on the part of the perpetrator. Dietz, Hepburn, and Stern (2007, pp. 3–4) note:

> One might also seek to justify emission reductions based on the weaker notion that emitters of greenhouse gases (past, present and future) have obligations—not arising from rights—to consider the climate damage caused, just like a passer-by might be morally obliged to aid someone who has taken ill, even though the ill person is unlikely to have a right to that assistance as such. [The moral and political philosopher Brian] Barry . . . constructs a theory of intergenerational justice that does not depend on equal rights across generations but only on the twin notions of "responsibility"—that "bad outcomes for which somebody is not responsible provide a *prima facie* case for compensation"—and "vital interests" . . . namely that there are certain objective requirements that all human beings have, regardless of their location in space or time.[2]

### 3. Ability-to-Pay Principle

"Emissions mitigation" refers to actions to reduce emissions. It imposes economic costs on countries that undertake such actions in terms of reduced consumption and growth. Most theories of justice would suggest that insofar as costs are imposed, more of them should be borne by

2. Dietz, Hepburn, and Stern (2007) quote Brian Barry, "Sustainability and Intergenerational Justice," in *Fairness and Futurity: Essays on Environmental Sustainability and Social Justice*, edited by Andrew Dobson (Oxford University Press, 1999), p. 97. There is also the issue of whether a country's responsibility should apply to the emissions it generates in production or in consumption (see Davis and Caldeira 2010; Pan, Phillips, and Chen 2008).

those whose incomes are greater. In a utilitarian view, in circumstances of diminishing marginal utilities—meaning that an additional unit of consumption and income forgone is more costly for a poor person than a rich one—world welfare will be maximized, or at least the loss in world welfare will be minimized, if those who are poorer incur lower costs. A Rawlsian perspective (based on the views of the political philosopher John Rawls) would, of course, be even more strongly redistributive. In terms of a carbon budget, therefore, most ethical perspectives would require future allocations to be inversely related to the ability (or, alternately, capacity) to pay for emissions reductions. This approach is also embedded in the Kyoto Protocol and reflected in the principle of common but differentiated responsibilities.

An extreme version of the capacity to pay—in the spirit of Rawls—is captured in the view that there should be no burden of payment for countries or individuals below a threshold level of income (Spence 2009; Chakravarty and others 2009; Bhagwati 2009b).[3]

## 4. Preserving Development Opportunities

The ability-to-pay principle focuses on adapting to the downside of emissions cuts by avoiding income losses for those with lowest incomes. But this has a more positive counterpart captured, for example, in the principle of the right to development enshrined in various United Nations initiatives. The right to development is really about preserving the economic opportunities for those who are currently poor—in this case by allocating to them sufficient carbon space in the future. A utilitarian perspective is that an extra unit of emissions and any resulting extra income will increase world welfare the most if it is allocated to the currently poor rather than to the currently rich.

---

3. The ability-to-pay argument has also been articulated in terms of international redistribution. According to Stern (2009b), "Any notions of equality and justice in the allocation of emissions rights should be embedded in a broad view of income distribution" (p. 155). The point here is that allocations of emissions rights are going to have enormous economic consequences, if not for the distribution of income at least for changes in this distribution. For example, if the cumulative carbon budget for the period 2010 to 2050 is, say, 750 gigatons, and the average future price of carbon is $50 per ton, climate change going forward will in effect involve distributing nearly $40 trillion. Thus, while some argue that climate change cannot be about addressing global poverty or redressing international income distribution, the magnitudes of funds involved will be large, dwarfing the size of current aid budgets.

Several contributions to the literature invoke the principle of the ability and capacity to pay and the related principle of preserving future development opportunities. Among these contributors are Baer, Athanasiou, and Kartha (2007), who have advocated the notion of greenhouse development rights (GDRs, the right to emit greenhouse gases based on their role in development) as well as Cao (2008), Frankel (2007), German Agency for Technical Cooperation (2004), Jacoby and others (2008), and Stern (2009b). Bosetti and Frankel (2009) make emissions cuts dependent on how far a country is from a certain per capita income threshold.

The economic opportunities principle is given high priority in Jacoby and others (2008), who explicitly construct a scenario in which future welfare of countries would not be compromised. Birdsall and Subramanian (2009) derive emissions allocations under several scenarios, each of which preserves developing countries' right to economic growth and energy use in the future (discussed in chapter 3).

## 5. Adjustment Costs

The clearest equity principles articulated in the literature as a basis for emissions allocations are those just discussed: equal per capita emissions, based on the idea that all people are created equal; historic responsibility, based on the idea of doing no harm to others or providing compensation for doing harm; ability to pay, based on basic notions of distributive justice; and preservation of future economic opportunities, based also on notions of distributive justice.

Some would argue that one or more of these four principles should be the only determinants of equitable allocations of emissions. But others have stated, suggested, or implied that so-called adjustment costs should also inform emissions allocations not necessarily because that would be equitable but in recognition of political realities (see Bosetti and Frankel 2009). Adjustment costs are the pain and disruption experienced by countries that have to make big emissions reductions. For example, if rich countries have to cut emissions by 80 percent over the next few decades, that would impose changes in behavior and lifestyle that will be costly. Is there an equity-based rationale for taking account of adjustment costs?

One of the few contributions to explicitly incorporate adjustment costs is Bosetti and Frankel (2009), who impose several adjustment-cost-related constraints on their modeling of emissions reductions. But the proposals in Stern (2007) and the UN Development Program (2007), which use 1990 as a base for calculating emissions reductions going forward, are implicitly "grandfathering" existing emissions allocations, and are in spirit attempting to give weight to adjustment costs by softening the impact of emissions reductions on those who have to make the largest reductions. It is worth noting here that the Stern (2007) and UN Development Program (2007) proposals are very close in spirit to the "contraction and convergence" ideas first proposed by Meyer (2000), which involve the global carbon budget's contracting consistent with climate change goals, with rich countries' emissions going down and poor countries' going up until they converge at a common emissions-per-capita target in the long run.

One argument supporting the inclusion of adjustment costs in equity calculations stems from a view that equity should pertain to changes made from a benchmark rather than levels and that there should be some rough parity in the economic and political pain caused by these changes. In a trade context, this is what Bhagwati has called "first-difference reciprocity": in trade negotiations, countries don't aim to equalize the level of tariffs but to broadly equalize changes in tariffs and consequent changes in market access. Adjustment-costs are likely to be greater and more compressed in time for countries that have to make larger cuts, which are likely to be countries with large emissions to start with. Implicit in the adjustment-costs principles is that the ability-to-pay principle, which gives much greater weight to the losses of the poor relative to the rich, should be qualified if the rich have to make large emissions reductions that would affect their economic situation.

## Equity for Whom? Individuals or Nations?

A critical dimension of equity is the unit of analysis. International cooperation on climate change takes place between countries, and so the country has to remain the unit of analysis. Most of the proposals in the literature start with the country as the unit of analysis in discussing equitable emissions allocations (Government of Brazil 1997; Bhagwati, 2009a; Government of India 2009; German Agency for Technical Cooperation 2004; Birdsall and Subramanian 2009; Kanitkar and others, 2010; Parikh and Parikh, 2009; Stern 2007; UN Development Program 2007).

Here, however, we start with the individual as the unit for any equity consideration (Cao 2008; Chakravarty and others 2009; Baer and others 2007). Ultimately, people have rights, and countries' rights and obligations derive from individuals (see Stern 2007). So our analysis will build from individuals to countries. The literature on equity in climate change has not recognized the importance of this distinction between the country and individual as the unit of analysis and therefore has not revealed an awareness of its consequences.[4]

The choice of the individual as a unit of analysis is not the same as adopting the equal per capita principle. Starting with the individual does, however, allow for the equal per capita principle to be one among several principles for allocating emissions. But the inclusion of other principles will typically result in a variation of per capita emissions across countries, that is, in departures from an equal per capita emissions outcome.

## Results

We now present results—the consequences for emissions allocations for countries—of the major proposals in the literature. We first highlight the consequences to major emitters of applying the individual principles. We then elaborate on the consequences of emissions allocations relative to business-as-usual for five proposals that are closely related to these individual elements.

The results we present in this section are all based on a sample of fifty countries that collectively account for about 94 percent of the world's emissions in 2008 and about 75 percent of the world's population.[5] The sample is based on an emissions threshold of 0.7 tons per capita and an income threshold of $2,000 per capita GDP in 2008, where income is measured in purchasing power parity (PPP). Broadly, we wanted to include the largest current and potentially largest future emitting countries that are likely to be key to achieving successful cooperation.

We assume, following the German Advisory Council on Global Change (2009), that the total cumulative carbon budget for fossil-based

---

4. Mattoo and Subramanian (2012) discuss in greater detail the differences between starting with the individual and with the country as the unit of analysis and the consequences of these different approaches for emissions allocations.

5. See Mattoo and Subramanian (2012) for details.

**FIGURE  2-3A.  Cumulative Emissions Allocations, by Country, 2010–50**

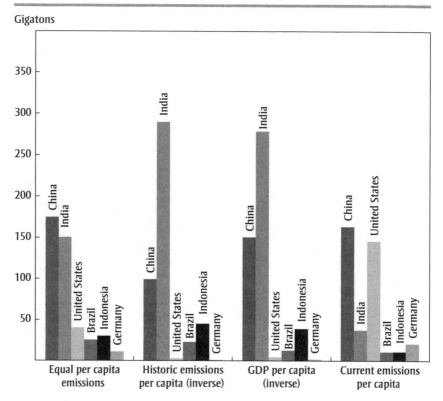

Source: Authors, based on analysis of data from the World Bank's World Development Indicators.

emissions for the period 2010 to 2050 is 750 gigatons. This amount would provide a 67 percent probability of meeting the 2 degrees centigrade "guardrail." If we assume that the share of the emissions for the countries in our sample remains broadly unchanged, this would imply a budget for our fifty-country sample of 704 gigatons.

## 1. Impact of Principles

First we spell out the implications of individual principles before describing the implications of proposals that are based on them. Figure 2-3a shows the impact of the individual principles on the total emissions that each country would receive. Figure 2-3b shows the impact on the per capita emissions allocated to each country.

**FIGURE 2-3B.** Cumulative Emissions Allocations per Capita, by Country, 2010–50

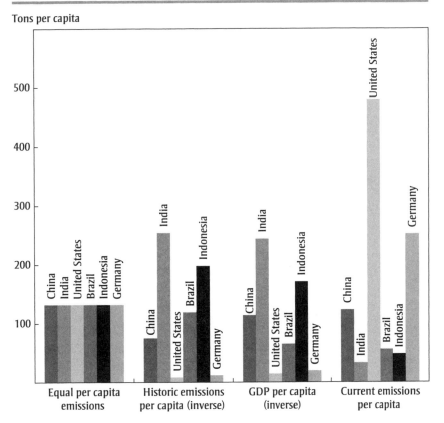

Tons per capita

Source: Authors, based on analysis of data from the World Bank's World Development Indicators.

Not surprisingly, different principles favor different countries in terms of the emissions allocations they would receive. China, India, and Indonesia benefit from, and the United States and European Union are hurt by, the historic-responsibility principle. Conversely, the United States and the EU receive greater emissions allocations when they are based on current emissions per capita, because it is this variable that captures adjustment costs and motivates some of the better-known proposals in the literature. Allocations based on GDP per capita favor the poorest countries, such as India and Indonesia (see figure 2-3b in particular). It is noteworthy that according to this principle China's higher income level results in India's getting over two times as much as China in emissions per capita. Under the ability-to-pay principle (figure 2-3b), too, income differentials between India and Brazil mean that India receives about three and a half times the emissions allocations per capita as Brazil. This translates into even larger differences in total emissions allocations because India's population is about six times the size of Brazil's (figure 2-3a).

Per capita allocations are very similar under the historic-responsibility and ability-to-pay principles. It is also noteworthy that both historic emissions and ability-to-pay principles yield greater per capita allocations than the equal per capita emissions principle does for countries such as India and Indonesia. For China and Brazil the converse is true: that is, they get greater per capita allocations under the per capita principle than under the historic-responsibility or ability-to-pay principles. This shows that as long as countries are poor—that is, far from converging to common levels of economic development—the poorer countries may be better off embracing principles other than the equal per capita principle.

## 2. Impact on Countries Relative to Business-as-Usual

So far we have compared the individual principles in terms of their implied emissions allocations for different countries. But countries will also be concerned with the impact of different proposals as compared to making no changes and continuing with business-as-usual. In figures 2-4a–e we compare the impact on different countries of five proposals: equal per capita emissions, historic responsibility, ability to pay, 80-20 cuts (where industrial countries reduce their overall emissions by 80 percent while developing countries reduce theirs by 20 percent), and preservation of future economic opportunities. Specifically, we compute the difference in the annual average emissions growth rate between each of the scenarios and the emissions growth rate under the business-as-usual scenario and plot this difference against the per capita GDP of countries.

We obtain emissions growth in the business-as-usual scenario from Birdsall and Subramanian (2009), which is optimistic about technology creation and dissemination in the business-as-usual situation. These technology assumptions are combined with those about population and per capita GDP to derive business-as-usual emissions growth.[6]

---

6. The per capita growth assumptions for all countries for the period from 2010 to 2050 are based on convergence (see Birdsall and Subramanian 2009).

**FIGURE 2-4.** Projected Average Annual Emissions Growth under Alternative Proposals as a Percentage of Business as Usual, between 2010 and 2050

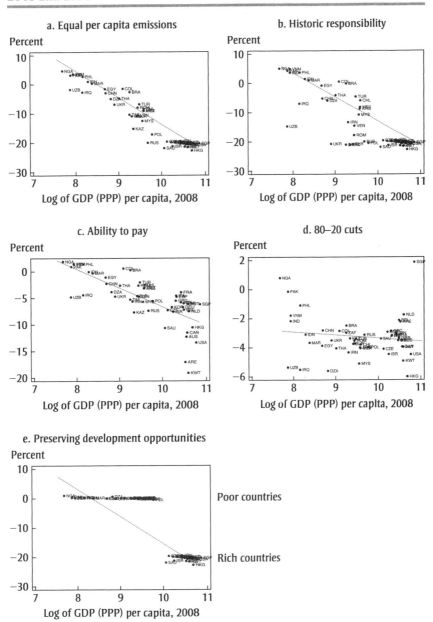

Source: Authors, based on analysis of data from the World Bank's World Development Indicators.

We specify the preservation of future economic opportunities principle in the following manner: we give all countries that have a per capita
GDP (PPP) in 2008 of less than US$20,000 their business-as-usual allo-
cations. This captures the graduation notion that people below certain
thresholds should not have to suffer any consequences (see Bosetti and
Frankel 2009). For countries above this threshold, we reduce their emissions allocations proportional to their business-as-usual levels so that the
global carbon budget is respected.

Several features stand out in these figures. First, most proposals are
broadly equitable in that they inflict smaller emissions growth cuts on
poorer countries, reflected in the significantly negative relationship with
current GDP per capita in the figures. The exception is the 80-20 cuts
proposal (figure 2-4d), which has a strong status quo bias. In fact, this
feature is common to some of the most influential contributions to the
literature that have focused on emissions cuts rather than allocations
(Stern 2007; UN Development Program 2007; Bosetti and Frankel 2009;
Jacoby and others 2008).[7] In Stern (2007) and UN Development Program (2007), which advocate the 80-20 cuts proposal, and in the Jacoby
proposal for 70-30 cuts, the baseline is 1990 emissions levels.

When the benchmark is some historical level of emissions, a cuts
approach tends to favor the status quo and hence preserves current
inequities. Consider, for example, the 80-20 cuts proposal of Stern and
the UN Development Program. At first blush, an 80 percent reduction
by the industrial countries and a 20 percent reduction by developing
countries relative to their 1990 emission levels appears strongly progressive. However, its real implications for equity are that poorer countries
lose substantially relative to their-business-as-usual path of emissions
(see figure 2-4d). A second feature that is illustrated in these figures
and table 2-1 is that a few large, poor countries—India, Indonesia, the
Philippines, Nigeria, Vietnam, and Pakistan—tend to receive consis-
tently high allocations. Any allocation that starts from the individual
as a unit of analysis and then aggregates to the level of countries on
the basis of population naturally favors large countries, which are on
average poorer. China, in contrast, experiences lower allocations in
nearly all scenarios because its per capita income is higher.

---

7. Kanitkar and others (2010) combine cuts with allocations.

**TABLE 2-1. Countries Least Adversely Affected under Different Proposals**[a]

| Equal per capita emissions | Historic responsibility | Ability to pay | 80-20 cuts | Preserving future development opportunities | |
|---|---|---|---|---|---|
| India | India | India | Singapore | China | Egypt |
| Indonesia | Indonesia | Indonesia | Pakistan | Russia | Malaysia |
| Brazil | Brazil | Pakistan | Nigeria | India | Pakistan |
| Pakistan | Pakistan | Nigeria | | Iran | Uzbekistan |
| Nigeria | Nigeria | Vietnam | | South Africa | Algeria |
| Vietnam | Vietnam | Philippines | | Mexico | Romania |
| Philippines | Philippines | Morocco | | Indonesia | Iraq |
| Colombia | | | | Brazil | Nigeria |
| Morocco | | | | Ukraine | Vietnam |
| | | | | Poland | Philippines |
| | | | | Turkey | Belarus |
| | | | | Thailand | Colombia |
| | | | | Kazakhstan | Chile |
| | | | | Venezuela | Morocco |
| | | | | Argentina | |

Source: Authors' compilation.

a. A country appears on the list if the emissions growth in each of the scenarios declines relative to the business-as-usual scenario by less than —0.5 percent.

One point that deserves emphasis concerns business-as-usual and the related proposals for the preservation of future economic opportunities. Business-as-usual emissions levels are closely related to future economic growth, which is based on some view about each country's prospects. Alternative growth projections have profound consequences for emissions allocations. For example, in the projections by the International Energy Agency (2009), growth is assumed to be 4.9 percent for China and 3.9 percent for India. In contrast, the Birdsall and others (2009) projections, based on assuming convergence, are 4.1 percent for China and 5.2 percent for India. Convergence has some empirical basis, but it also has normative appeal in that it leaves room for higher potential growth for those who are currently poorer.

## Conclusions

Even as the world contemplates stronger action to reduce $CO_2$ emissions to prevent catastrophic climate change, how this goal can be accomplished equitably has become central to the debate. In this chapter we have presented an analytical framework to encompass the existing contributions to the literature on equity in climate change. We have sought, in particular, to highlight the consequences of different approaches to equity for future emissions allocations.

There seems to be a shared recognition that the pattern of today's emissions is unbalanced. Today, rich countries have substantially greater per capita $CO_2$ emissions than poor countries, reflecting substantially higher usage of energy per capita. There is less agreement on how equity considerations should inform future action to allocate emissions in order to head off or mitigate climate change, and this lack of consensus is reflected in the different proposals that have been made.

Four equity-based principles and related proposals recur in the literature. These suggest that emissions allocations (1) be allocated equally on a per capita basis; (2) be inversely related to historic responsibility for emissions; (3) be inversely related to ability to pay; and (4) be directly related to future economic opportunities. The case has also been made for taking account of adjustment costs in emissions allocations.

At first blush, each of the principles discussed here seems to merit inclusion in any determination of equitable emissions allocations. Thus, privileging any one principle or a subset of principles to the exclusion of others does not seem justified. But after due consideration of all principles, there may well be a reason to favor just one principle: the preservation of future economic opportunities. Why?

Taken in isolation, the adjustment-costs principle, which motivates formulating equity in terms of emissions cuts, tends to favor the status quo. Even reasonably progressive cuts relative to historic levels—for example the 80-20 cuts proposal that implicitly accords primacy to adjustment costs—tend to favor large current emitters such as the United States, Canada, Australia, the oil exporters, and China, at the expense of the low emitters. Cuts relative to business-as-usual tend to favor countries, particularly China, for whom the greatest growth is forecast, when such forecasts are based on recent economic performance.

Other principles—equal per capita emissions, historic responsibility, and ability-to-pay—favor some poor and populous developing countries such as India, Indonesia, the Philippines, Pakistan, and Nigeria. Going forward, in any purely equity-based approach these countries would not be required to assume onerous commitments to reduce emissions.

However, these equity principles would hurt not just industrial countries but other developing countries. Thus, a weakness of these proposals is that they would inflict unjustified economic costs on some poor countries that would not receive the emissions allocations they need to sustain growth. At the same time, the generous allocations provided to the poor and populous countries in excess of their growth needs would amount to unjustified largesse because then climate change would become an instrument for redressing unrelated inequities.

A weakness of these proposals is that on the one hand they would inflict unjustified economic costs on a large number of poor countries that would not receive emissions allocations needed to sustain likely growth rates, but on the other they would provide allocations to some countries in excess of their growth needs.

The principle of "preserving future development opportunities" is most appealing because it corresponds most closely to the notion that developing countries should not be constrained in the future by a problem that they did not largely cause in the past. The climate change problem has imposed a hard "carbon budget" constraint on humanity. In the absence of climate change, there would not have been such a constraint. The key equity question is whether this hard budget constraint should bite for developing countries by curtailing their future economic opportunities and their growth and energy needs. And the answer seems to be that it should not: not just because they are poor but also because they did not cause much of the problem.

If we assume that incomes of different countries tend to converge over time, which has both some empirical support and normative appeal, then developing countries have the greatest economic opportunities. Preserving these opportunities would require emissions allocations to all developing countries close to their projected business-as-usual levels. This principle minimizes conflicts among developing countries. It also has the virtue of not making climate change an instrument for income redistribution for reasons unrelated to climate change. However, the burden of meeting climate change goals would then fall entirely on industrial countries, which would be obliged to make drastic cuts in emissions, especially if China's large business-as-usual emissions have to be accommodated and compensated for by cuts by more developed countries. The resulting economic contraction of industrial countries would in turn have negative feedback effects on developing countries because of compromised trade and finance.

Hence, one key and broad point that emerges from this review is that in discussions of equity in emissions allocations, conflicts of interest are both inherent and strong, perhaps irreconcilably so. They are inherent because the exercise is about allocating a fixed aggregate carbon budget. They are strong because the budget is not really fixed but shrinking dramatically, especially when viewed in relation to the growing needs of developing countries. Science demands drastic compression in aggregate emissions in order to achieve a reasonable probability of keeping temperatures below reasonable levels. Given current rates of technological progress, the available carbon budget is not even adequate to sustain business-as-usual growth rates for developing countries, let alone for the world as a whole. The required cuts would only be small enough to be politically acceptable if there were radical—historically unprecedented—technological breakthroughs that allowed significantly higher levels of growth and energy consumption that kept a lid on emissions.

It may, therefore, be desirable to shift the emphasis of international cooperation toward generating a low-carbon technology revolution. In such a revolution, equity would still have a key in shaping such international cooperation, but a different one from that described in earlier scenarios. Equity would be less about mediating the allocation of a fixed emissions pie than about informing the contributions of different countries in generating a low-carbon technology revolution so as to enlarge this pie, that is, achieving the same emissions from greater and more technologically efficient growth. Such a revolution can transform climate change into a non-zero-sum game and offers perhaps the only hope of reconciling the development needs of low-income countries with the climate change goals of humanity.

**APPENDIX TABLE 2-1. Equity Principles Proposed in the Climate Change Literature[a]**

| Principles→ Papers↓ | Equal per capita emissions | Historic responsibility | Ability to pay | Preserving development opportunities | Adjustment costs |
|---|---|---|---|---|---|
| Agarwal and Narain (1991) Saran (2009) Ghosh (2009) | Y | Y | | | |
| Antholis (2009) | N | | | | |
| Baer, Athanasiou, and Kartha (2007) | | Y | Y | | |
| Bhagwati (2009a, 2009b) | | Y | | | |
| Birdsall and Subramanian (2009) | | | | Y | |
| Bosetti and Frankel (2009) | | Y | Y | | |
| Cao (2008) | | Y | Y | | |
| Chakravarty and others (2009) | | | Y | | |
| Cooper (2008) | | Y | Y | | |
| Frankel (2007) | Y | Y? | Y | Y | |
| German Advisory Council on Global Change (2009) | Y | Y | Y | | |
| German Agency for Technical Cooperation (2004) | Y | Y | Y | | |
| Government of Brazil (1997) | | Y | | | |
| Jacoby and others (2008) | Y | | Y | Y | |
| Joshi and Patel (2009) | | | | Y | |
| Kanitkar and others (2010) | Y | Y | | | |
| Meyer (2000) | Y | | | | |
| Müller, Höhne, and Ellermann (2007) | | Y | | | |
| Pan et al. (2008) | | Y | | | |
| Panagariya (2009) | | Y | | | |
| Parikh and Parikh (2009) | Y | Y | | | |
| Posner and Sunstein (2008) Posner and Weisbach (2010) | N? | | Y? | | |
| Spence (2009) | | | Y | | |
| Stern (2009c) | | Y | Y | | Y? |
| Stern (2009b) | | | | | |
| UN Development Program (2007) | | | | | Y |
| Winkler, Brouns, and Kartha (2006) | | Y | Y | | Y |

Source: Authors' compilation.
a. Y = Yes; N = No; Y? = qualified support; blank cells mean that the authors did not discuss that option.

# 3 | Preserving Development Opportunities

Earth provides enough to satisfy every man's need, but not every man's greed.
—Mahatma Gandhi

The review of the equity literature in chapter 2 suggested the recurrence of five ethical principles for determining the allocations of emissions across countries. We argued that the principle of preserving future development opportunities had considerable appeal because it is closest to the notion that developing countries should not be constrained in the future by a problem that they did not largely cause in the past. The problem that was caused in the past by industrial countries matters to the extent that it constrains future opportunities.

But how should this principle be formalized and quantified to derive emissions allocations for different countries? In this chapter we attempt to answer this question. We propose an approach to emissions allocation that is grounded in three principles.

1. *Focus on growth and energy, not on emissions per se.* First and foremost, we submit that from an ethical perspective, what is fundamental is not the right to pollute; it is people's ability to grow and become richer. To the extent that these two are distinct, the fundamental right should encompass access to basic energy-based amenities such as meal preparation at home, pleasant ambient temperatures indoors, and access to transportation, all at reasonable cost, regardless of

geographical location. Economic growth and equitable or comparable access to energy-based services, not emissions, should be the touchstone of planned emissions allocations.[1]

2. *Take history as guide to growth and equitable access.* Our second key point is that the right to growth and energy services should be determined by a simple historical rule: in developing countries, growth and access to energy services (not to emissions) should be the same as it was in developed countries at comparable levels of income per capita. The rationale: It seems unfair for people in developing countries to be deprived of access merely because they are latecomers to the development process in the sense that others have already used up a key resource for development. To give a simple example, access to air conditioning or cooking gas should be the same for a household in Chennai, India, as it was in Austin, Texas, when the United States had a per capita income comparable to that of current-day India.[2]

3. *Future technologies as basis for carbon efficiency.* Third, the mistakes of the past must not be repeated. In developing countries, energy needs should be met by the most efficient technology, not by the technology used by advanced countries at comparable stages of development. For example, the Chennai household's air conditioning in 2025 should not run on the same technology as the Austin household's in, say, 1990. Instead, it should be very similar to the Austin household's in 2025 (or an even more advanced technology if India can leapfrog over the United States in technological development).

Making growth and energy access, not emissions, the touchstone for emissions allocation brings the development dimension back into the climate change conversation in a way that was envisaged in the 1992 Rio Declaration on Climate and Development, which called for common but differentiated responsibilities among countries. It also has the advantage

---

1. Of course, the magnitude of allocations will have to be in line with the critical constraint of not heating the planet beyond critical tipping points. But allocations should primarily be driven by objectives.

2. One problem with this principle is it implicitly advocates replicating the historical errors made by rich countries in an era of low carbon prices. For example, cheap energy may have facilitated location of production and consumption; families' migration from New England to Texas may have become feasible because of cheap air conditioning. As we note later, going forward it will be in the interest of developing countries to avoid the public policies and practices that created incentives that led to these errors.

of avoiding a number of problems that the emissions-based approach has created.

In the next section of this chapter we discuss the basic approach and data. In the following section we quantify the historical relationships between development and energy consumption per capita, $CO_2$ efficiency in production, and $CO_2$ efficiency in consumption. In the penultimate section we provide projections of $CO_2$ emissions in 2050 under three scenarios, reflecting our basic approach. In the last section we discuss the implications of our analysis and present conclusions.

## Distinguishing between Energy Use and Efficiency of Emissions

The three principles argue for making a distinction between the consumption of direct energy-related services and the efficiency of $CO_2$ emissions generation in production and consumption activities.[3] This distinction yields three relevant variables:

1. Energy use per capita: the energy to "produce" road travel and electricity generation
2. Emissions from consumption per unit of energy consumed: the carbon intensity of energy consumption
3. Emissions in production per unit of GDP: the carbon intensity of energy production (increases in the carbon intensity in consumption and production signal greater inefficiency)

Each of these variables has a different historic relationship to development. Table 3-1 presents some basic energy use (residential electricity use and vehicle use) and emissions data for 2005, disaggregated along these lines. The results show the following:

—For all countries, emissions from production still account for the bulk of total emissions.

—The share of total emissions related to consumption is substantially greater for industrial countries (about 42 to 43 percent for the United States, France, and the UK) than for India (22 percent) and China (14 percent).

---

3. Excluding emissions caused by deforestation, for which there are inadequate data.

**TABLE 3-1. Selected Indicators Related to Emissions, 2005**

| Country | (1) Total emissions (MtCO$_2$)[a] | (2) Emissions per capita (tCO$_2$ per person) | (3) Share of consumption in total emissions (percent) | (4) Energy use per capita (tons of oil equivalent [TOE] per person) | (5) Carbon intensity of consumption[b] (tCO$_2$/TOE) | (6) Carbon intensity of production (MtCO$_2$/KtOE)[c] |
|---|---|---|---|---|---|---|
| Bangladesh | 36.34 | 0.24 | 0.36 | 0.09 | 7.48 | 0.39 |
| Denmark | 47.51 | 8.77 | 0.33 | 1.36 | 6.07 | 0.12 |
| Philippines | 76.42 | 0.90 | 0.33 | 0.16 | 7.21 | 0.52 |
| Pakistan | 118.40 | 0.76 | 0.32 | 0.24 | 6.12 | 0.73 |
| Malaysia | 138.04 | 5.38 | 0.27 | 0.55 | 7.07 | 0.74 |
| Netherlands | 182.95 | 11.21 | 0.31 | 1.30 | 6.61 | 0.20 |
| Turkey | 218.93 | 3.04 | 0.30 | 0.39 | 6.40 | 0.42 |
| Brazil | 329.28 | 1.76 | 0.30 | 0.29 | 0.77 | 0.26 |
| South Africa | 330.34 | 7.04 | 0.21 | 0.59 | 10.96 | 1.07 |
| Indonesia | 340.98 | 1.55 | 0.30 | 0.35 | 10.67 | 0.83 |
| Australia | 376.78 | 18.47 | 0.32 | 1.76 | 12.07 | 0.35 |
| France | 388.38 | 6.38 | 0.42 | 1.58 | 0.94 | 0.11 |
| Mexico | 389.42 | 3.78 | 0.37 | 0.54 | 7.86 | 0.32 |
| Italy | 454.00 | 7.75 | 0.35 | 1.03 | 5.68 | 0.17 |
| United Kingdom | 529.89 | 8.80 | 0.43 | 1.43 | 6.20 | 0.14 |
| Germany | 813.48 | 9.86 | 0.40 | 1.51 | 6.54 | 0.17 |
| India | 1,147.46 | 1.05 | 0.22 | 0.17 | 17.13 | 1.11 |
| Japan | 1,214.19 | 9.50 | 0.28 | 1.09 | 5.18 | 0.19 |
| China | 5,100.60 | 3.91 | 0.14 | 0.33 | 11.76 | 1.94 |
| United States | 5,816.96 | 19.62 | 0.43 | 3.00 | 7.61 | 0.27 |

Source: Birdsall and Subramanian (2009, p. 21).
a. MtCO$_2$ = million tons carbon dioxide.
b. Household electricity consumption.
c. Kt = kilotons.

**FIGURE 3-1.** Carbon Intensity of Production, Selected Major
Emitters, 1960–2005

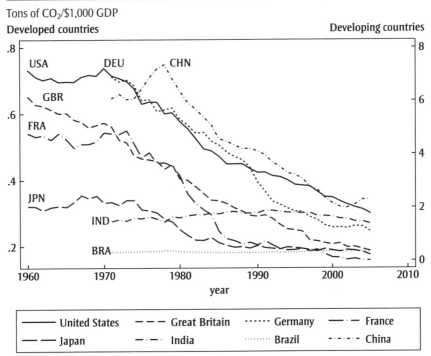

Tons of $CO_2$/\$1,000 GDP

Source: Birdsall and Subramanian (2009, p. 32).

—Industrial countries have made good progress in production efficiency, measured as $CO_2$ emissions generated in production as a share of
GDP (see figure 3-1).

—India is about four and a half times as inefficient as the United States
in production and even more so compared to some European countries
(see table 3-1, column 6).

—China is almost twice as inefficient as India. Viewed historically,
countries such as India do not appear to be doing badly in terms of both
the level and trajectory of $CO_2$ emissions.

—India and China are less inefficient on the consumption side
(see table 3-1, column 5).

—The greatest disparities arise in energy consumption per capita
(see table 3-1, column 5):

　　—U.S. per capita energy consumption is about nine times that of
　　China and eighteen times that of India.

**FIGURE 3-2.** **Energy Use per Capita, Selected Major Emitters, 1960–2005**

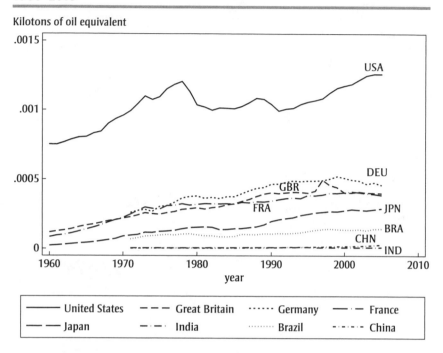

Kilotons of oil equivalent

Source: Birdsall and Subramanian (2009, p. 34).

—Even the less profligate European countries consume substantially greater amounts of energy per capita than China and India.

If one plots consumption of energy use per capita for selected rich and poor countries,[4] one finds the following (see figure 3-2):

—Consumption of energy per capita appears to have been rising slowly, especially in the United States.

—It is also rising in Brazil, though from relatively low levels compared to those of the high-income United States and lower-income China. Brazil's low emissions may be the result of its reliance on ethanol as vehicle fuel.

Plotting carbon intensity of consumption for selected countries yields the following (see figure 3-3):

4. We use country-specific weighted averages of transport and road emissions in figures 3-2 and 3-3.

**FIGURE 3-3.** Carbon Intensity of Consumption, Selected Major
Emitters, 1960–2005

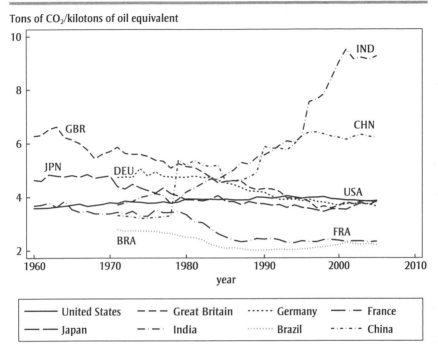

Tons of CO$_2$/kilotons of oil equivalent

Source: Birdsall and Subramanian (2009, p. 33).

—Consumption intensity has been increasing in China and India.

—Consumption emissions intensity has been increasing with income in China, India, and Brazil, although it is still below levels in the United States and other rich countries, where it appears to have stabilized.

## Historical Relationships between Energy and Emissions and Development

We estimate the historical relationship between energy use and emissions efficiency in production and consumption, on the one hand, and development on the other. The principle of preserving future development opportunities for developing countries will run up against the question of how these opportunities can be pinned down or quantified.

And our response is that future energy access must be related to future income for developing countries just as energy access was related to income for industrial countries. This seems a reasonable and ethical way of quantifying future development opportunities related to energy consumption. For production efficiency, we need historical relationships, but we use them slightly differently: we posit that the relationship between production efficiency and development in the future for developing countries cannot be the same as the relationship in the past for industrial countries because technology keeps improving. At least some of these technological improvements will be passed on to developing countries.[5] The key findings are as follows:

—Developing countries are still far more carbon-intensive in their production than are developed countries.

—In virtually all countries, the trend is in the direction of greater efficiency. Carbon intensity in production decreases as income increases.

—There are also efficiency gains, though more modest, in terms of emissions associated with consumption. In developed countries, recent income growth seems to drive efficiency, but in developing countries, it contributes to inefficient practices, though not significantly.

—In marked contrast, energy *use* in both sets of countries is still rising almost as fast as income, particularly in developing countries.

—In developed countries, use is less affected by income growth than in developing countries and is trending down, perhaps because people are conserving with income growth, either using less energy directly (turning down the thermostat) or investing to insulate and using less energy for the same degree of warmth.[6] The implication is not surprising; energy services are a normal good, and we should expect demand for them to rise with income—and apparently somewhat faster at lower levels of income where "needs" have been less fully met.

5. For a detailed discussion of our econometric exercise involving the estimation of these historic relationships, see Birdsall and Subramanian (2009).

6. For a detailed explanation of the methodology used to make these projections see Birdsall and others (2009, appendix 2). We could distinguish between these two possibilities only if we had a measure of the energy service outcome ("warmth"), but we have only a measure of the energy service input (household use of energy in kilotons of oil equivalent [KtOEs]).

# Projecting Emissions in 2050 under Alternative Scenarios

On the basis of these historical relationships, we project emissions in 2050 under various scenarios.[7] Before we do so, we need to elaborate on a key factor that enables us to formalize future development opportunities. Projecting future emissions requires estimates of these historical relationships. Birdsall and Subramanian (2009, appendix 2) have developed equations that capture these relationships. But we also need projections of GDP. The relationships suggest on an intuitive level how much emissions will change as GDP changes, but to get total emissions we need to pin down how GDP itself will change.

What is a fair or ethically justifiable way of projecting future growth? Future economic growth has typically been predicted on the basis of some view about each country's prospects, as in many projections by the International Energy Agency (2009) and Cline (2007). These are necessarily subjective and typically tend to extrapolate from the recent past.

Alternatively, one might simply say that projecting growth over a long horizon should be a more objective supply-side exercise. The simplest premise for doing so is economic convergence, namely, the assumption that all countries would tend in the long run to converge to similar standards of living and that future *growth* rates will be inversely related to current *levels* of per capita income. The postwar evidence is that the major carbon emitters, especially those in Asia, have shown signs of convergence, although not all countries have done so. This means that the use of current levels of GDP is appropriate as a predictor of future growth rates (see Barro and Sala-i-Martin 2005 and Caselli 2004 for evidence of convergence). More recently, in the period from 2002 to 2008 leading up to the recent global financial crisis, the phenomenon of convergence has become more widespread, with nearly 70 percent of countries growing faster than the United States (Subramanian 2011). In any case, it is appealing to use convergence not just as a predictor of future growth but also as a normative basis for preserving the growth opportunities of the poorest countries. That is, the convergence principle is fair and historically consistent because it implies that future growth should

---

7. An important caveat here is that clearly, emissions reductions efforts will themselves have a feedback effect on growth, which we do not incorporate. More broadly, capturing many of these effects will require a fully specified dynamic model that is beyond the scope of this chapter. Our aim is to highlight broad principles and effects rather than to precisely identify the relevant magnitudes.

be determined by a country's current level of income. For example, if Japan in 1950 grew at 6 percent, then a country that in 2010 is as poor as Japan was in 1950 should also be expected to grow at the same rate as Japan. Thus, our growth assumptions and our energy access assumptions treat all countries the same in "development time."

### Business-as-Usual Scenario

In the baseline, business-as-usual (BAU) scenario, we find that rich countries' emissions will increase by about 70 percent and poor countries' emissions by over 200 percent from the 1990 baseline year (table 3-2).[8]

In this scenario, we can back out what might be called a notional or a benchmark equitable-burden-sharing rule for rich and poor countries. This is done by estimating how much rich countries would have to reduce emissions, given the BAU emissions profile for poor countries, and the fact that global emissions must decline by 50 percent relative to 1990 levels to prevent environmental catastrophe.

This reduction amount serves as a benchmark because it identifies how much rich countries would have to do—or undo—to ensure that the development potential of poor countries is not compromised or constrained because of the past actions of rich countries. Equitable burden sharing in the BAU scenario would require rich countries to cut their emissions by 270 percent (Birdsall and Subramanian 2009, table 6). That is, for developing countries to continue on a relatively unconstrained development path, rich countries would have to go not just to zero emissions but beyond zero emissions, and actually contribute negative emissions, for example, by means of reforestation that adds to the carbon absorption capacity of the atmosphere. This may be unrealistic and even impossible in practice, but it serves the purpose of showing that the 80-20 emissions reduction rule currently under discussion would seriously constrain development in poor countries, despite seeming to put the greater burden of future emissions reductions on the rich countries.

Under the equitable-burden-sharing rule in the BAU scenario, which is still very demanding in assuming that developing countries will continue to increase carbon efficiency, China and India would *increase* their emissions relative to 2005 levels by about 61 percent and 240 percent,

---

8. Details of projecting emissions in the baseline or business-as-usual (BAU) scenario are provided in Birdsall and Subramanian (2009, appendix table 3).

**TABLE 3-2.** **Emissions in 2050 in Selected Countries
under Business-as-Usual Scenario, Compared to 2005
(Listed by Volume of Total 2005 Emissions)**

| Country | Total $CO_2$ emissions (millions of tons) | | Per capita $CO_2$ emissions (tons) | |
|---|---|---|---|---|
| | 2005 | 2050 | 2005 | 2050 |
| United States | 5,817 | 8,333 | 19.7 | 20.2 |
| China | 5,101 | 8,225 | 3.9 | 5.8 |
| Russia | 1,544 | 1,562 | 10.8 | 14.9 |
| Japan | 1,214 | 945 | 9.5 | 8.4 |
| India | 1,147 | 3,909 | 1.1 | 2.4 |
| Germany | 813 | 834 | 9.9 | 10.5 |
| Canada | 549 | 690 | 17.0 | 16.9 |
| United Kingdom | 530 | 612 | 8.8 | 9.0 |
| Korea | 496 | 462 | 10.3 | 9.2 |
| Italy | 454 | 397 | 7.7 | 8.2 |
| Iran | 446 | 1,082 | 6.5 | 10.1 |
| Mexico | 389 | 992 | 3.8 | 7.0 |
| France | 388 | 432 | 6.4 | 6.5 |
| Australia | 377 | 496 | 18.5 | 18.1 |
| Spain | 342 | 337 | 7.9 | 8.0 |
| Indonesia | 341 | 1,156 | 1.6 | 3.9 |
| South Africa | 330 | 536 | 7.0 | 11.9 |
| Brazil | 329 | 784 | 1.8 | 3.2 |
| Saudi Arabia | 320 | 733 | 13.8 | 13.9 |
| Ukraine | 297 | 429 | 6.3 | 13.5 |
| Poland | 296 | 378 | 7.7 | 11.3 |
| Turkey | 219 | 535 | 3.1 | 5.4 |
| Thailand | 214 | 596 | 3.3 | 7.3 |
| Netherlands | 183 | 181 | 11.2 | 10.4 |
| Egypt | 161 | 543 | 2.1 | 4.3 |
| Kazakhstan | 155 | 247 | 10.2 | 17.4 |
| Venezuela | 142 | 363 | 5.4 | 8.2 |
| Argentina | 141 | 403 | 3.6 | 7.5 |
| Malaysia | 138 | 543 | 5.4 | 12.7 |
| Pakistan | 118 | 840 | 0.8 | 2.4 |
| Czech Republic | 118 | 99 | 11.6 | 11.1 |
| Belgium | 112 | 120 | 10.6 | 11.2 |
| Uzbekistan | 110 | 486 | 4.2 | 12.5 |
| United Arab Emirates | 110 | 204 | 27.0 | 33.1 |
| Iraq | 97 | 587 | 3.4 | 9.1 |
| Greece | 96 | 91 | 8.6 | 8.9 |
| Romania | 91 | 141 | 4.2 | 7.9 |
| Algeria | 84 | 644 | 2.6 | 12.6 |
| Hong Kong | 81 | 267 | 11.9 | 31.1 |
| Vietnam | 80 | 298 | 1.0 | 2.4 |

*(continued)*

**TABLE 3-2.** **Emissions in 2050 in Selected Countries under Business-as-Usual Scenario, Compared to 2005 (Listed by Volume of Total 2005 Emissions) (Continued)**

| Country | Total $CO_2$ emissions (millions of tons) | | Per capita $CO_2$ emissions (tons) | |
|---|---|---|---|---|
| | 2005 | 2050 | 2005 | 2050 |
| Kuwait | 77 | 154 | 30.3 | 31.9 |
| Austria | 77 | 75 | 9.4 | 9.8 |
| Philippines | 76 | 341 | 0.9 | 2.4 |
| Israel | 69 | 120 | 10.0 | 11.1 |
| Belarus | 61 | 90 | 6.2 | 11.8 |
| Colombia | 60 | 188 | 1.4 | 2.8 |
| Chile | 59 | 130 | 3.6 | 5.7 |
| Nigeria | 55 | 662 | 0.4 | 2.2 |
| Singapore | 43 | 49 | 10.1 | 9.1 |
| Morocco | 41 | 195 | 1.4 | 4.1 |

Source: Birdsall and Subramanian (2009, p. 27).

respectively. Their corresponding emissions per capita in 2050 would be 5.8 and 2.4 tons per capita (see table 3-2).

These are the relevant numbers that should inform the debate on equitable burden sharing. They are a radical departure from the current view that developing countries should *cut* their emissions by 20 percent.

### Current-Technology-Frontier Scenario

The term "current technology frontier" refers to the best performance today in relation to the carbon efficiency of consumption and production and energy use per capita. When we project emissions in this scenario, we assume that in the period from 2005 to 2050, all developed countries reach the frontier of carbon efficiency in consumption and production, and also reach the frontier level of restraint in energy consumption. Currently, Germany is the best performer in terms of efficiency levels in consumption and production; Australia is the best performer in terms of energy use. We assume that developing countries' efficiency parameters will follow those of the most efficient developed countries.

Here, we continue to assume that the direct consumption energy-related needs of poor countries are as in the BAU scenario, that is, equitable burden sharing involves no reduction in the energy needs of

**TABLE 3-3. Final Parameter Values and Associated Emissions Reductions, Percent Change from 1990 Levels**

| | Parameters | | | | | | CO₂ reduction (percent change from 1990)[a] | | | |
| | Alpha | | Gamma | | Beta | | By income group | | | |
| Scenario | Rich | Poor | Rich | Poor | Rich | Poor | Rich | Poor | Global | Equitable for rich |
|---|---|---|---|---|---|---|---|---|---|---|
| Business-as-usual | -1.5 | -1.1 | -0.1 | -0.1 | 0.6 | 0.9 | -48 | -189 | -112 | 251 |
| Current technology frontier | -2.1 | -1.7 | -0.5 | -0.5 | -0.3 | 0.9 | 12 | -47 | -15 | 132 |
| Avoiding catastrophe | -4.1 | -3.7 | -1 | -1 | -0.3 | 0.9 | 53 | 47 | 50 | 53 |

Source: Birdsall and Subramanian (2009, p. 23). Alpha denotes the responsiveness of carbon efficiency in production to changes in income; gamma, of carbon efficiency in consumption; and beta, of changes of energy use also to changes in income.

a. A negative reduction implies an increase in emissions. The final column specifies the equitable reduction for the rich countries, that is, what sort of reduction would be required by the rich alone in order to meet the emissions target of a 50 percent emissions reduction by 2050. Compare this with the value in the "Income Group CO₂ reduction" column.

developing countries but remains the same as in the BAU scenario. This assumption is, of course, at the heart of our equity principle.

Assuming that all countries operate at the highest possible levels of efficiency and energy usage, total emissions still rise by nearly 47 percent in developing countries and decline by 12 percent in the rich countries. Global emissions rise by 15 percent. In this scenario, an equitable-burden-sharing rule would require the rich to decrease emissions by 132 percent.

### Avoiding Catastrophe Scenario

Neither the business-as-usual nor the current-technology-frontier scenario comes close to meeting the target for reducing global emissions by 50 percent by 2050. Indeed, they both imply emissions continuing to rise. In the "avoiding catastrophe" scenario we ask what improvements in the efficiency parameters are necessary in rich countries that, if also adjusted rapidly in developing countries, would deliver the global emissions reductions target of 50 percent by 2050.

To ensure a total reduction of 50 percent, we assume massive improvements in technology in the developed countries and considerable catching up in the developing countries through technology transfer and their own technological breakthroughs. We continue to assume that poor countries' energy consumption services are not compromised.

Table 3-3 shows that very large improvements in the efficiency parameters in both developed and developing countries are necessary to meet the global target consistent with avoiding a climate change catastrophe. Compared to the BAU scenario, the elasticity of the carbon intensity of production to income in developed countries would have to decline by 2.6 percentage points, from −1.5 to −4.1, and the elasticity of energy use to income would have to decline by 0.9 percentage points, from 0.6 to −0.3.

How large are these required changes? One way to assess whether they are even possible is to ask whether the industrial countries have ever achieved similar gains in the past. The oil price shock of the early 1970s, when energy prices quadrupled, is a natural place to seek an answer.

We estimated how the carbon intensity of production and energy use responded to income for periods before and after that oil shock. We find that production efficiency improved substantially: before the shock a one-percentage-point increase in GDP led to a 0.1 percent reduction in the energy/GDP ratio; after the shock a one-percentage-point increase in GDP led to a 1 percent decrease in the same ratio. However, the improvements in energy use from the oil shock were far more modest.

This exercise, though merely illustrative, nevertheless serves to confirm that even with the massive energy price changes of the early 1970s, the improvement in efficiency was far short of what will be required in the future if global emission targets are to be met.

## Summary and Conclusions

In this chapter we present three principal points. We have sought to give flesh to the principle of preserving development opportunities, which means essentially the right to economic growth and access to energy to fulfill basic needs. We showed that quantifying development opportunities on these two dimensions pointed to a kind of historical consistency: poor countries' future growth and energy access should be no different from that enjoyed by the currently rich at a comparable stage of their development.

Second, we quantified historical relationships between energy needs and the efficiency of energy use in production and consumption, on the one hand, and development on the other. One conclusion is that carbon efficiency gains have responded to "development," in the form of reduced emissions intensity of GDP, as countries have become richer. But gains in conservation as countries have developed have been more elusive.

Our third point relates to the results of our projections exercise. Our key finding is that improvements in technology at rates consistent with those we observed historically, even for the most carbon-efficient economies among major emitters, provide little hope of meeting the broadly agreed global target for emissions reductions of 50 percent of 1990 levels by 2050. Proposals such as the 80-20 cuts proposed in recent discussions such as Stern (2007) and the United Nations Human Development Report (UN Development Program 2007), which appear to be progressive and equitable, in fact are highly inequitable. For developing countries to preserve their future development opportunities, their emissions would have to grow by over 200 percent, and in this case developed countries would have to reduce emissions by about 270 percent.

This suggests that any prospect of meeting the aggregate global emissions target that is consistent with developing countries' not sacrificing their energy needs will require revolutionary improvements in technology on both the production and consumption sides far greater than any seen historically, and certainly greater than the changes seen after the oil price shocks that led to large increases in the price of energy and carbon. Only with these improvements and their worldwide diffusion would the current 80-20 emissions-reductions distribution advocated by Lord Nicholas Stern and the UN Development Program be equitable and hence politically acceptable. Otherwise this burden-sharing rule would almost surely be inequitable by our definition: even a 20 percent emissions reduction in developing countries would require lower pure energy use for given income by their citizens than the level historically enjoyed by people in developed countries at the same income level.

Given the critical importance of achieving substantial technology gains, the world needs to go on a war footing to meet this goal. (How international cooperation should inform such a low-carbon technology revolution is discussed in chapter 1.)

# 4

# Can Global Emissions Reductions Inhibit Developing-Country Industrialization?

Minimising the cost of necessary emissions cuts and containing the disruption they will cause requires setting the right price for carbon emissions: it must be high, and the same everywhere.
—"The Deal We Need from Copenhagen," *FT.com*, November 2, 2009

Everything is second-best, at best.
—Avinash Dixit, "Governance Institutions and Economic Activity," 2009

The focus of discussions on climate change mitigation has been on how much emissions should be cut and how developing countries should be compensated for any cuts they make. Accordingly, much of the literature has focused on the aggregate costs to countries of mitigation actions, and the transfers that would be necessary to maintain welfare in the poorer parts of the world. However, the structural implications of these actions have received less attention.

In this chapter we seek to make a twofold contribution. On outcomes, we focus on manufacturing exports as well as on manufacturing output both in the aggregate and in selected sectors. On policy, we isolate the impact of three distinct actions: emissions reductions alone; emissions tradability; and international transfers.

Why the focus on manufacturing? If it were unambiguously clear that manufacturing had no special role in the development process and did not generate positive growth externalities, there would be no need to focus on manufacturing. An analysis focusing on the aggregate effects of climate change actions would then be sufficient. But the literature is unclear on the role of manufacturing in economic development. Some economists argue in favor of the positive growth benefits from manufacturing output and exports while others are more skeptical.[1] We do not espouse either view, but if manufacturing does matter, policy-makers will want to take that into account, and this necessitates an analysis that disaggregates the effects of different policies, and that is what we provide in this chapter.

Policy disaggregation is useful because each dimension of policy may have different effects and may affect different countries differently. For example, the impact of emissions reductions per se varies across countries depending on the carbon intensity of their production. Furthermore, the financial flows that arise from tradability themselves have structural consequences and need to be evaluated. The rich literatures on the impact of aid on growth, and of financial globalization on growth, do not reach unambiguous conclusions: many studies find either some positive or no effects, whereas others suggest that under some conditions both public and private transfers may have negative effects on growth.[2] In this chapter we seek to contribute to this debate by providing some evidence on the structural impact of transfers.

The literature on the costs of climate change mitigation is voluminous and includes a number of important contributions (Cline 2007; Nordhaus 2007; Stern 2007; UN Development Program 2007; World Bank 2009). This literature recognizes that a regime that favors static efficiency through uniform global prices for carbon and hence energy can be inequitable; consequently, this literature typically recommends financial and technology transfers to alleviate the adverse effects on developing countries (Stern 2007; World Bank 2009). Hardly explored in this literature is the potential tension between static efficiency and dynamic effects stemming from changes in the composition of output and exports in developing countries as a result of uniform global prices.

---

1. Recent proponents of this view include Jones and Olken (2008) and Rodrik (2009).

2. The skeptical view of the impact of aid on growth can be found in Brautigam and Knack (2004), Collier (2007), Djankov, Montalvo, and Reynal-Querol (2005); Easterly (2007), Moyo (2009), Easterly, Levine and Roodman (2004), Elbadawi (1999), Knack (2001), Prati and Tressel (2006), Rajan and Subramanian (2008, 2011). The skeptical view of the impact of financial globalization on private net flows and on growth can be found in Gourinchas and Jeanne (2007); Prasad, Rajan, and Subramanian (2007); and Rogoff and others (2004).

The fact that transfers can themselves accentuate this tension through Dutch-disease-type effects, while acknowledged (Strand 2009), has also not been fully explored.[3] We focus on the case where developing countries cut their emissions so that by 2020 they are 30 percent less than projected business-as-usual levels (China already plans a 20 percent cut in energy intensity), which it is hoped will then lead industrial countries to cut their emissions by 30 percent in 2020 from their 2005 levels. This reflects the European Union's current position.[4] We also consider a broad range of other scenarios.

Our main empirical findings, which come with a number of important caveats, are the following. Some currently high-carbon-intensity countries and regions—China, India, Eastern Europe and Central Asia, and the Middle East and North Africa—will experience substantial reductions in manufacturing output and exports from emissions reductions alone. For a subset of these countries, especially China and India, these effects will be aggravated by emissions tradability and transfers. For these countries the negative effects will be substantial, not just on carbon-intensive manufacturing but also on other manufacturing sectors. For example, for China and India, the aggregate effect of all these policy actions would be a decline in manufacturing output of 6 to 7 percent, and in manufacturing exports of 9 to 11 percent. These effects would be aggravated if these developing countries pursued more ambitious emissions targets. There could

3. Dutch disease is the negative impact on an economy of anything that gives rise to a sharp inflow of foreign currency, such as the discovery of a natural resource, which leads to currency appreciation, making the country's other products less price-competitive on the export market. It also leads to higher levels of cheap imports and can lead to deindustrialization as industries apart from resource exploitation are moved to cheaper locations. The phrase refers to the Dutch economic crisis of the 1960s following the discovery of North Sea natural gas.

4. See European Commission, "What Is the EU Doing about Climate Change?" *Climate Action* (http://ec.europa.eu/clima/policies/brief/eu/index_en.htm): "For 2020, the EU has committed to cutting its emissions to 20% below 1990 levels. This commitment is one of the headline targets of the Europe 2020 growth strategy and is being implemented through a package of binding legislation. The EU has offered to increase its emissions reduction to 30% by 2020 if other major emitting countries in the developed and developing worlds commit to undertake their fair share of a global emissions reduction effort."

also be transitional dislocation costs as resources are reallocated across sectors.

In contrast, the manufacturing sector in low-carbon-intensity countries such as Brazil and the Rest of Latin America will be less affected by actions related to climate change. In the case of sub-Saharan Africa, effects might even be positive, although any boost to manufacturing exports could be reduced through transfers and the consequent Dutch-disease-type effects.

These findings could have implications for the positions that countries will adopt in international negotiations. There is a strong consensus among economists that the best way forward is to get a uniform global carbon price—via either a common global tax or international emissions trading—supplemented with financial transfers to address the equity dimension of climate change. This article of faith in the policy community was captured by an editorial in the *Financial Times,* which stated, "Minimising the cost of necessary emissions cuts and containing the disruption they will cause requires setting the right price for carbon emissions: it must be high, and *the same everywhere.* . . . In the actual world, a global scheme of tradable emissions quotas is the best solution" (emphasis added).[5]

If there are no positive externalities from shrunken manufacturing exports and output, this view would have considerable merit because individual countries and international cooperative efforts have to deal with only one externality—the carbon externality. But if climate change actions affect long-run growth by affecting manufacturing, two externalities, carbon and growth, will have to be reconciled in ways we discuss briefly in the final section of this chapter.

This chapter is organized as follows. In the next section we describe the emissions reductions scenarios that we believe have greatest relevance for policy, and briefly discuss the positions that the United States and the European Union have taken on a key issue, the international tradability of emissions rights. In the following section we present the results of our quantitative simulations of each of the scenarios. In the last section, "Discussion and Conclusions," we assess the implications of our results.

---

5. "The Deal We Need from Copenhagen," *FT.com,* November 2, 2009.

## The Scenarios

To facilitate understanding the implications of alternative policy combinations, we have constructed a set of scenarios. The key policy data in each scenario is the magnitude of emissions reductions by each major country or country group. This magnitude is based on the stated policy positions of different players and is common to all the scenarios considered here. The scenarios differ in other dimensions of policy: whether international emissions tradability is allowed and whether international private and public transfers take place.

### Emissions Cuts Only Scenario

In our first scenario, by 2020 developed countries cut their emissions by 30 percent relative to their 2005 levels and developing countries cut their emissions by 30 percent relative to levels as they would have been in 2020 in the business-as-usual, or reference, scenario, in which no cuts in emissions are made.[6] Developed countries' 30 percent reduction reflects the EU's announcement that it would be willing to implement this higher cut if other countries also participated in cooperative action.[7] Developing-country reductions reflect recent statements of intent. For example, China recently announced that it plans to extend the pledge announced in its last five-year plan to cut energy use per unit of economic output by 20 percent.[8] India, too, has announced a range of initiatives, even though it has not yet announced a quantitative target.[9] We also consider a range of cuts by developing countries to test the robustness of our results.

### Scenarios Involving Trading of Emissions Rights

Recent initiatives envisage, in addition to emissions cuts, international tradability of emissions rights. We envisage that an international agreement to cut emissions will lead to a certain allocation of emission rights

---

6. This would entail agreeing on a hypothetical baseline for emissions. However, what matters most is setting a legal ceiling on the absolute magnitude of emissions.

7. European Commission, "What Is the EU Doing about Climate Change?"

8. Harvey Morris, Fiona Harvey, and Geoff Dyer, "Beijing in Pledge to Spur Energy Efficiency," *Financial Times,* September 23, 2009.

9. See Ghosh (2009) and Government of India, Ministry of Environment and Forests (2009).

across countries. If these rights are allocated within countries through market-based mechanisms, such as auctions, a national price for emission rights will be established, with higher prices in countries that undertake bigger reductions. (The same outcome would be observed if some countries imposed a higher carbon tax than other countries.) If emissions rights were internationally tradable, then potential users in high-price countries would purchase emission rights from holders in low-price countries. If such trade were not restricted, it would continue until prices across countries were equalized. (The same outcome would be observed if all countries imposed the same level of carbon tax). Private purchases of emissions rights lead to private financial flows from initially high-price countries to initially low-price countries. (No such flows would arise if all countries imposed carbon taxes at the same level.)

Two bills regarding emissions trading have been proposed in the House and Senate of the United States Congress. The bills differ slightly.[10] In the House bill, the maximum amount of total emissions rights that can be traded internationally would be one-half of the 2 billion tons of $CO_2$ that can be traded, with the remaining half being traded domestically. In the Senate version, a maximum of one-quarter of the 2 billion tons can be traded internationally.[11]

The Council of the European Union has recently moved in favor of international tradability. It would like to see "preferably by no later than 2015, a robust OECD-wide carbon market through the linking of cap-and-trade systems which are comparable in ambition and compatible in design, to be extended to economically more advanced developing countries by 2020."[12]

10. The House bill was the American Clean Energy and Security Act of 2009 (ACES) introduced in the 111th United States Congress (H.R. 2454), by Representatives Henry A. Waxman of California and Edward J. Markey of Massachusetts, both Democrats. It passed the House of Representatives on June 26, 2009, but died in the Senate. The Senate bill was the Clean Energy Jobs and American Power Act, also introduced in the 111th United States Congress (S. 1733) by Senators John Kerry and Barbara Boxer, both Democrats, but was not passed.

11. The Senate bill also has a stipulation that after 2018, one and a quarter international offset credits would be required to equal one allowance of domestic offset credit.

12. Council of the European Union (2009).

In order to capture the effects of both emissions cuts and tradability, we consider four policy scenarios.

1. NTER—stands for No Tradable Emissions Rights. In this first scenario, described earlier, emissions cuts are implemented by each country but there is no trade in emissions rights and there are no international financial transfers.

2. TER1—stands for Tradable Emissions Rights but with no Private Financial Flows. In this scenario, countries cut emissions and emissions rights are internationally tradable. International arbitrage leads to a uniform global carbon price, as explained earlier. However, in order to consider the effects of price equalization separately from the effects of the private financial flows resulting from international trade in emission rights, we assume in this scenario that these latter flows do not take place. Thus, the TER1 scenario is equivalent to the imposition of a uniform global carbon tax regime with each country retaining revenues domestically.

3. TER—Tradable Emissions Rights with Private Financial Flows. In this scenario, countries cut emissions, emissions rights are internationally tradable, and we allow the associated private financial flows to take place. The TER scenario is equivalent to a uniform global carbon tax regime with revenues transferred across countries from those who would have had higher carbon taxes to those who would have had lower.

4. TERWMT—Tradable Emissions Rights with Mitigation Transfers. Supplementary public transfers are made to compensate developing countries so that they attain the same welfare levels as in the business-as-usual case. The political infeasibility of generating support for large public transfers to countries such as China and India might make this seem unrealistic. But we use this scenario primarily as an illustrative benchmark and also to show the impact of public transfers on some of the poorer countries in sub-Saharan Africa, for whom large public transfers do remain politically feasible.

## Quantifying Economic Effects under Cooperative Emissions Reductions

Empirical research offers few good answers to many of the policy questions that are the subject of this chapter. As in the case of the trade policy issues addressed in the next chapter, an econometric approach seems handicapped by the absence of past events and our inability to construct experiments that are comparable with the policy changes of greatest interest. In situations of simultaneous policy changes of the kind that we consider in this chapter, in which there could be significant interaction effects among different countries, and where we are interested in quantifying the effects of these changes on output and trade in different sectors of the economy, a computable general equilibrium (CGE) approach seems appropriate. The model used in this chapter is the same as that in the previous chapter and is subject to the same caveats and limitations (see Mattoo and others 2009a for details).

In this section we discuss the effects of different policy scenarios to developing countries. Even within developing countries, the impact of emission reductions is likely to differ between regions where the carbon intensity of production is high and those where it is relatively low. Carbon intensity of production is measured as tons of carbon emitted per million dollars of output. To facilitate our analysis we divide countries and regions into three groups by the carbon intensity of their production:

1. The high-carbon-intensity group. Countries with economywide carbon intensities higher than 500 tons per million dollars—includes China, India, Russia, and the Rest of Eastern Europe and Central Asia (ECA).[13] It possibly includes the Middle East and North Africa (MENA), at 380 tons per million dollars.[14]

2. The relatively low-carbon-intensity group. Countries with economywide carbon intensities lower than 200 tons per million dollars—clearly includes Brazil and the Rest of Latin America (LAC).

3. An intermediate group. Countries with economywide carbon intensities between 280 and 332 tons per million dollars include those in Sub-Saharan Africa (SSA), Rest of South Asia (SA), and Rest of East Asia (EA).

The first group of countries—we focus especially on China and India—is likely to be subject to the most significant effects from emissions reduc-

---

13. These acronyms are based on the World Bank's regional groupings.

14. Production could be relatively carbon-intensive in developing countries for these broad Global Trade Analysis Project (GTAP) categories, both because individual products are produced more carbon-intensively and because the broad product categories include more carbon-intensive products.

tions. We then describe how effects differ for the second group, focusing on Brazil, and finally turn to the intermediate group, focusing on sub-Saharan Africa. (See table 4-1 for the impact of the various scenarios on emissions reductions and table 4-2 for the impact on welfare, output, and trade.)

### Category 1: High-Carbon-Intensity Countries

Here we consider the impact on this group of countries in each of the four scenarios described in the previous section. In the NTER scenario, in which cuts are implemented without the possibility of international trade in emission rights, our simulations suggest that the average carbon price would go to $92 per ton in low- and middle-income countries (LMICs), compared to $478 per ton of carbon in high-income countries.[15] Aggregate welfare would fall by 2.2 percent relative to the baseline in all LMICs, with relatively small reductions in the large emitters such as China and India and larger welfare losses in the oil-exporting regions such as Russia and the Middle East (see table 4-2).

Total manufacturing exports decline by 4.5 percent in China and 7.3 percent in India. The corresponding declines in manufacturing output are 2.9 percent and 3.7 percent (see table 4-2).[16] The main reason for these declines is that manufacturing is the most carbon-intensive sector, after the energy sector itself, and so is worst hit by increases in carbon price.

In the second scenario (TER1), in which we assume that there are no private financial flows, tradability per se leads to a uniform global carbon price of $133 per ton. This scenario is equivalent to a uniform global carbon tax regime where the taxes are retained domestically. In this case,

---

15. All prices are measured in dollars per ton of carbon. The price per ton of $CO_2$ can be obtained by dividing the carbon price by approximately 4 (or, more precisely, by $44/12 \approx 3.67$).

16. Russia is an exception in this group of countries because its manufacturing output and exports increase in the NTER scenario. The reason is that when all countries cut their emissions, there is a significant contraction in global demand for energy; energy accounts for a large share of the Russian economy—53 percent of its exports and 24 percent of its output (see Mattoo and others 2009a, appendix table 8, "Share of Output by Sector, [% of Total Output, 2004]). The contraction in demand induces a significant shift in resources away from Russia's energy sector and toward other sectors, including manufacturing.

**TABLE 4-1. Impact of Various Scenarios on Emissions Reductions**

| Scenario | World total emissions cuts | High-income countries | United States | EU | Low- and middle-income countries | China | Brazil | India | Sub-Saharan Africa |
|---|---|---|---|---|---|---|---|---|---|
| Percent change in emissions relative to business-as-usual in 2020 | | | | | | | | | |
| NTER | −33.8 | −40.9 | −43.9 | −40.9 | −30.0 | −30.0 | −30.0 | −30.0 | −30.0 |
| TER1 | −33.8 | −18.8 | −21.4 | −14.8 | −41.9 | −50.5 | −14.9 | −38.0 | −42.3 |
| TER | −33.8 | −42.3 | −21.5 | −15.0 | −41.8 | −50.4 | −15.0 | −38.0 | −42.3 |
| TERWMT | −33.8 | −42.0 | −21.8 | −15.5 | −41.6 | −50.4 | −15.0 | −37.9 | −42.0 |
| Percent change in emissions relative to 2005 | | | | | | | | | |
| NTER | 14.5 | −26.5 | −30.0 | −30.0 | 54.3 | 97.3 | −5.0 | 78.0 | 24.0 |
| TER1 | 14.5 | 0.4 | −1.9 | 1.1 | 28.0 | 39.6 | 15.6 | 57.6 | 2.2 |
| TER | 14.5 | 0.2 | −2.1 | 0.8 | 28.2 | 39.9 | 15.4 | 57.7 | 2.3 |
| TERWMT | 14.5 | −0.2 | −2.4 | 0.1 | 28.6 | 39.8 | 15.4 | 58.0 | 2.8 |

Source: Mattoo and others (2012).

**TABLE 4-2. Impact of Scenarios on Countries' Welfare, Manufacturing Output, and Exports, Expressed as the Size of the Change Compared to Business-as-Usual in 2020**

| Scenario | World total emissions cuts | High-income countries | United States | EU | Low- and middle-income countries | China | Brazil | India | Sub-Saharan Africa |
|---|---|---|---|---|---|---|---|---|---|
| Percent change in welfare | | | | | | | | | |
| NTER | -1.5 | -1.2 | -1.3 | -1.3 | -2.2 | -1.8 | -1.5 | -1.4 | -1.9 |
| TER1 | -0.9 | -0.2 | -0.2 | -0.1 | -2.6 | -3.8 | -2.1 | -0.5 | -2.0 |
| TER | -0.9 | -0.5 | -0.7 | -0.4 | -1.7 | -1.5 | -1.5 | -0.8 | -1.5 |
| TERWMT | -0.8 | -1.2 | -1.1 | -1.4 | 0.0 | 0.0 | 0.0 | 0.0 | 0.0 |
| Percent change in output of total manufacturing | | | | | | | | | |
| NTER | -1.7 | n.a. | -1.3 | -0.7 | -2.5 | -2.9 | -3.7 | -0.8 | 1.8 |
| TER1 | -1.6 | n.a. | 0.0 | 0.5 | -4.0 | -5.8 | -5.2 | 0.6 | -5.2 |
| TER | -1.5 | n.a. | 0.8 | 0.7 | -4.4 | -6.5 | -5.5 | 0.6 | 0.7 |
| TERWMT | -1.4 | n.a. | 1.6 | 1.3 | -5.0 | -7.0 | -6.1 | -0.2 | 0.3 |
| Percent change in exports of total manufacturing | | | | | | | | | |
| NTER | -2.9 | -2.4 | -2.3 | -1.9 | -3.5 | -4.5 | -7.3 | -1.5 | 5.8 |
| TER1 | -1.8 | 0.2 | 0.1 | 1.2 | -3.9 | -5.8 | -8.6 | 2.0 | 3.5 |
| TER | -1.9 | 1.6 | 2.7 | 2.6 | -5.6 | -9.4 | -10.7 | 2.7 | 2.3 |
| TERWMT | -1.9 | 3.9 | 5.0 | 6.5 | -8.3 | -11.7 | -15.4 | -0.7 | -1.0 |

Source: Mattoo and others (2012).

welfare losses increase substantially, especially for China, from 1.8 percent to 3.8 percent, and for India from 1.5 percent to 2.1 percent (see the TER1 scenario in table 4-2). Manufacturing output declines further, to 5.8 percent in China and 5.2 percent in India.

As expected, allowing transfers along with tradability alleviates the welfare declines seen in the nontradability scenario (scenario TER in table 4-2).[17] However, it magnifies the impact, especially on manufacturing exports via Dutch-disease-type mechanisms. For example, China's manufacturing exports fall by 9.4 percent and India's by 10.7 percent. The pure effect of the private transfers—the difference between the TER1 and TER scenarios—is to induce a further decline in exports: 3.6 percent for China and 2.1 percent for India.[18]

Other high-carbon-intensity countries in the Middle East and North Africa and the Rest of Eastern Europe and Central Asia suffer output and export reductions due to the emissions reductions, just like China and India. But the former group does not suffer much from emissions tradability and the implied private transfers. The magnitude of transfers will depend on the wedge between the domestic carbon price prevailing after emissions cuts and the uniform global price that will prevail with tradability. These two prices will be close for the Middle East and North Africa and the Rest of Eastern Europe, so that tradability leads to a small price change and hence also to a small private transfer.

If developing countries were to receive additional official transfers to compensate for the loss of welfare caused by emissions reductions, then the Dutch-disease-type effects would be even stronger (see the TERWMT scenario in table 4-2). Manufacturing exports would decline by 12 percent for China and 15 percent for India. The corresponding figures for manufacturing output are 7 percent and 6 percent. As we mentioned earlier, these transfers are unlikely to materialize for the larger developing

---

17. The magnitude of this effect depends on the quota allocation scheme.

18. In our model, Dutch-disease effects from transfers arise mainly from the condition that the external accounts must be balanced, which is a plausible description of long-run equilibrium. Are these effects from transfers plausible? In the case of China, the results suggest that a transfer of about 1.8 percent of GDP would depress manufacturing export growth by about 0.5 percent. This is well within the range obtained from econometric estimates. Rajan and Subramanian (2011) find that a 1 percent increase in the aid-to-GDP ratio tends to reduce overall manufacturing growth by close to 1 percent.

**FIGURE 4-1.** Impact of Emissions Reductions by All Developing Countries on China's Manufacturing Exports and Output Relative to Business-as-Usual in 2020

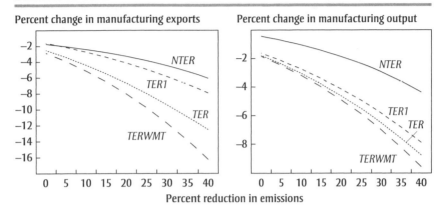

Source: Mattoo and others (2012).
NTER = No tradable emissions rights
TER1 = Tradable emissions rights but with no private financial flows
TER = Tradable emissions rights with private financial flows
TERWMT = Tradable emissions rights with mitigation transfers

countries but cannot be ruled out for poorer countries. To maintain welfare, the EU, Japan, and the United States would be required to make total public and private transfers equal to about 1 percent of their GDP—a figure similar to the recent demands for transfers made by developing countries.

In sum, emissions limits with tradability create a dilemma for this group of countries: tradability leads to a contraction in the manufacturing sector, and the more the country seeks to maintain the welfare status quo, the higher the price it will pay in terms of further contraction of this sector.

**Generalizing the Results to Other Scenarios**    Are these results unique to the assumptions we have made about the extent of emissions reductions by developing countries? In figures 4-1 and 4-2 we show the consequences of replicating the analysis described in the previous section for a range of emissions reductions by developing countries—from no emissions reduction (relative to BAU) to a 40 percent cut to keeping the emissions reduction by high-income countries fixed at 30 percent below 2005 levels. For China and India, for example, we find results consistent with the findings described earlier.

**FIGURE 4-2. Impact of Emissions Reductions by All Developing Countries on India's Manufacturing Exports and Output Relative to Business-as-Usual in 2020**

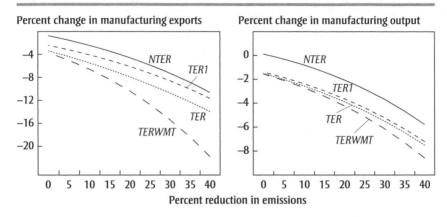

Source: Mattoo and others (2012).
Key: See figure 4-1.

Several features are noteworthy about these figures. First, as expected, the greater the emissions reductions by these countries the greater the decline in their manufacturing exports and output. More interesting are the consequences of tradability and transfers, which are captured by the gap between the different lines in the graphs.

For *exports,* significant adverse impacts arise from the Dutch-disease-type effects of transfers. Note in figures 4-1 and 4-2 the difference between TER1, which involves no transfers, and TER, which allows private transfers, or TERWMT, which allows also public transfers. For China, the incremental effect of private transfers increases with the level of emissions reductions (the gap between the TER and TER1 scenarios widens).[19] Note that a 40 percent emissions reduction relative to business-as-usual still represents an increase in emissions relative to 2005. If developing countries had to start ensuring even stabilization of carbon

19. The magnitude of transfers for any country is the product of the international price of carbon and its own sales and purchases of emissions. The international price rises with deeper emissions cuts by developing countries. The sales and purchases will depend on the wedge between the domestic and international price of carbon. In the case of China, this wedge narrows more gradually—hence the volume of its emissions sales declines gradually—because of its greater carbon intensity.

emissions by 2020, the implied effects on manufacturing exports, based on extrapolating the trends shown in figures 4-1 and 4-2, would be enormous.

For *output,* the significant adverse effects arise from the economy-wide carbon price-increasing effects of tradability (see in figures 4-1 and 4-2 the difference between NTER, which assumes emissions are not tradable, and TER1, which assumes emissions are domestically trad-able). In fact, even if India and China made no cuts in emissions but kept emission levels to business-as-usual levels and allowed inter-national tradability, each would see a decline in manufacturing output of about 1.5 percent.

### Category 2: Low-Carbon-Intensity Countries

The effects on low-carbon-intensity countries' manufacturing sectors from policy actions related to climate change are likely to be different from the effects on high-carbon-intensity countries. Two factors coun-teract each other. On the one hand, any change in the price of carbon affects manufacturing output and competitiveness less in these countries because of their low carbon intensity. For example, Brazil's total carbon intensity of $168 per ton is about one-quarter of China's and one-third of India's. On the other hand, reductions in emissions require progres-sively higher carbon price increases in these countries, in large part because their production is already relatively clean and it is harder for them to squeeze out deeper and deeper reductions. For example, to achieve a 5 percent emissions reduction, Brazil's carbon price would need to be $43, but to achieve a 30 percent reduction in emissions, Brazil's carbon price would need to increase to $376 per ton of carbon, more than four times the required level in India, and nine times the required level in China.

When a developing country such as Brazil makes only small cuts in emissions, the positive effect on the manufacturing sector of its relatively low carbon intensity dominates the negative effect of its higher carbon price (see figure 4-3, NTER scenario). But when larger cuts are made, the converse is true—the large increases in carbon price overwhelm the ben-efits of low relative carbon intensity so that in Brazil, for example, man-ufacturing exports and output decline. If trade in emissions rights is allowed, Brazil enters the market at low levels of emissions reductions as a seller but at higher levels of emissions reductions as a buyer—like the

**FIGURE 4-3.** **Impact of Emissions Reductions by All Developing Countries on Brazil's Manufacturing Exports and Output Relative to Business-as-Usual in 2020**

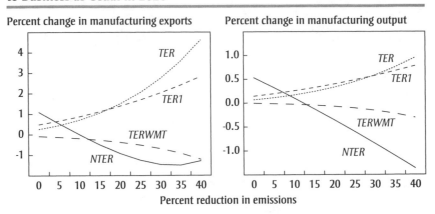

Source: Mattoo and others (2012).
Key: See figure 4-1.

high-income countries. The result in the latter situation is a decline in the carbon price toward the global uniform price and private outflows, both of which benefit the manufacturing sector (see figure 4-3, TER1 and TER scenarios).

### Category 3: Intermediate-Carbon-Intensity Countries

The impact of emissions reductions by all developing countries on intermediate-carbon-intensity countries in sub-Saharan Africa, Rest of South Asia, and Rest of East Asia is approximately midway between the impact on the high- and low-carbon-intensity economies. We focus here on sub-Saharan Africa.[20] If all developing countries cut their emissions by 30 percent, the sub-Saharan manufacturing sector actually expands (see figure 4-4, NTER scenario). The primary reason is these countries' low carbon intensity in manufacturing, which, combined with the lower emissions tax that follows from emissions reductions, actually improves sub-Saharan countries' competitiveness relative to other countries'.

20. East Asia resembles Brazil in that emissions reductions require a high carbon price due to their already relatively clean production. Therefore, emissions trading leads to a decline in the carbon price, which benefits manufacturing.

**FIGURE 4-4.** **Impact of Emissions Reductions by All Developing Countries on Sub-Saharan Africa's Manufacturing Exports and Output Relative to Business-as-Usual in 2020**

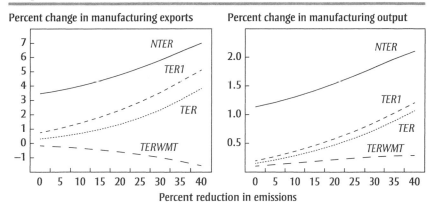

Percent change in manufacturing exports

Percent change in manufacturing output

Percent reduction in emissions

Source: Mattoo and others (2012).
Key: See figure 4-1.

However, if sub-Saharan countries receive large public transfers to compensate for loss in welfare (1.5 percent), then they could experience an adverse export effect from a Dutch-disease-type mechanism. The negative effect of transfers on manufacturing exports (the gap between the TER and TERWMT scenarios in figure 4-4) could be close to 4 percent, unless these transfers were successfully invested in ways that enhanced productivity in manufacturing or reduced the costs of conducting international trade, such as improving ports and airports.

### Changes in the Composition of Manufacturing

It is clear that the bigger impacts are in energy-intensive manufacturing, but countries may also be interested in the impacts on other manufacturing sectors, including clothing, electronics, and transport equipment. The trade-off between carbon intensity and long-run growth effects could vary across these sectors. For example, if the dynamic growth effects are weaker in energy-intensive sectors than in other manufacturing sectors, and if the latter are not substantially affected by emissions reductions and emissions tradability, international commitments on emissions reductions should raise fewer growth concerns.

In China and India and other countries like them, the impact of emissions reductions and tradability on the category "other manufacturing" will also be substantial (see Mattoo and others 2009a). Output will decline by 5 percent for China and 3.3 percent for India, and exports by close to 7 percent for both countries. For Brazil, East Asia, and sub-Saharan Africa, the impact on the output of other manufacturing sectors will be relatively modest. It is noteworthy that Dutch-disease-type effects will remain strong for exports of other manufacturing sectors in China, India, and sub-Saharan Africa. The effect of private transfers is to induce a decline in exports of 3.7 percent for China and 2.4 percent for India, respectively. For sub-Saharan Africa, the effect of private and public transfers is to induce a 5.2 percent decline in other manufacturing exports.

Overall, the preceding results suggest that the interests of developing countries might diverge when it comes to some of the key issues in the climate change negotiations. The differences between countries in terms of the impact on the manufacturing sector are the following. High-carbon-intensity countries (China, India, Eastern Europe and Central Asia, the Middle East and North Africa) will be more resistant to emissions reductions than low-carbon-intensity countries (Brazil, Latin America, East Asia) because of the impact on both manufacturing output and exports. Some high-carbon-intensity countries, especially China and India, will also be resistant to emissions tradability because of the further negative impact on output and of the impact of the resulting private transfers on manufacturing exports. Low-carbon-intensity countries will not be averse to emissions tradability. For sub-Saharan African countries, a potential negative effect could stem from the effect of public transfers on manufacturing exports, unless these transfers could be successfully invested in ways that enhanced productivity in manufacturing or reduced trade costs.

## Cost of Dislocation

So far we have focused on the impact of emissions reductions on the composition of output and exports. There are also likely to be dislocation costs as resources are reallocated across sectors, and the nature of these dislocations will differ between high- and low-income countries. For example, in the United States and the EU, all nine manufacturing sectors in our model are likely to expand as a result of international tradability of emissions, whereas in China, eight of the nine sectors are expected to see a decline in output (refined oil, chemicals, rubber and plastics, paper products and publishing, mineral products, ferrous metals, other metals, transport equipment, and other manufacturing). In India, seven out of the nine sectors are likely to see a decline in output. In the model we assume that factors of production can move easily across sectors, but if some factors of production, such as labor and capital, are sector-specific and imperfectly mobile, then the transition to any new equilibrium could lead to at least temporary unemployment. The irony is that high-income countries, such as the European Union and the United States, which typically have better social protection mechanisms, are less likely to need to deal with the contraction of tradable sectors—sectors whose output is exportable or importable.

## Discussion and Conclusions

As more countries accept the need for action on climate change, both the prospects for and the impact of cooperative emissions reductions are receiving significant attention. In this chapter we have provided a methodological tool with which we have attempted to quantify the impact of cooperative policy actions related to climate change on the manufacturing sector in developing countries. We depart from the existing work on climate change in two ways. First, we have disaggregated the policy actions into emissions reductions alone, international emissions tradability, and international transfers. Second, in terms of outcomes, instead of focusing on aggregate economic output, we quantify the effects on manufacturing output and exports.

These distinctions are important for a number of reasons. The heterogeneity of developing countries means that different types of policy action may have different effects and a disaggregation is crucial to understanding this heterogeneous response. The focus on the manufacturing sector and subsectors stems from the need to take into account the possibility that manufacturing output and exports could affect long-run growth performance.

Our key findings are the following. Some currently high-carbon-intensity countries and regions (China, India, Eastern Europe, Central Asia, the Middle East, and North Africa) will experience substantial reductions in manufacturing output and exports from emissions reductions alone. For a subset of these countries, especially China and India, these effects will be aggravated by emissions tradability (especially on manufacturing output) and transfers (especially on manufacturing exports). For this subset, the negative effects will be substantial not just for carbon-intensive manufacturing but also other manufacturing sectors.

In contrast, the manufacturing sector in low-carbon-intensity countries such as Brazil and Latin America will be minimally affected by the actions related to climate change. In the case of sub-Saharan Africa, effects might even be positive, although any boost to manufacturing exports could be reduced through transfers and the consequent Dutch-disease-type effects. Of course, if private and public transfers are able to raise productivity and reduce trade costs, then these effects could be offset.

These findings could have implications for the positions that countries adopt in international negotiations on climate change. If there are no positive externalities from manufacturing exports and output, policy choices are simpler because individual countries and international cooperative efforts have to deal with only one externality, the carbon externality. But if climate change actions, by affecting manufacturing, affect long-run growth, two externalities, carbon and growth, will have to be reconciled.

For low-carbon-intensity countries, the results suggest that there is little tension between the two externalities because the impact of climate change actions on the manufacturing sector is limited. For sub-Saharan Africa, there might be a tension related to transfers, which would need to be addressed.

But for high-carbon-intensity countries (especially China, India, Eastern Europe, Central Asia, the Middle East, and North Africa), whose manufacturing exports and output will be substantially affected, the choice may be more difficult. This choice can have several dimensions. For example, countries will have to determine where, specifically, the long-run growth externality resides. If it is primarily in non-energy-intensive manufacturing sectors, developing countries can justifiably resist international obligations that adversely affect these sectors. If energy-intensive sectors also have positive long-run benefits, the reconciliation between the carbon and growth externalities becomes more difficult.

A second dimension relates to policy instruments. If two externalities need to be addressed, two policy instruments will need to be deployed. The first-best solution might then be to tax the carbon externality appropriately by taking on international obligations on emissions reductions and tradability, while addressing the manufacturing externality through a combination of production subsidies (if the externality lies in manufacturing output) or export subsidies (if the externality lies in manufacturing exports). For developing countries, this first-best solution will encounter two problems. First, World Trade Organization rules prohibit the use of export subsidies, and production subsides can be legally countervailed by trading partners. Unless these rules are relaxed, the first-best response is not possible. A second, arguably bigger, problem is the difficulty of implementing subsidies: the experience with industrial policies and "picking winners" has highlighted the demanding requirements for successfully doing so. Thus, if implementation capacity is limited and countries find themselves in a second-best world, the reconciliation of the two externalities becomes more difficult.

In this second-best world, one option for countries would be to use one instrument but to strike a balance between the two objectives. So if countries cannot implement subsidies to capture the growth externality, they may choose to allow some increase in carbon prices (consequent upon, say, domestic emissions reductions) but not to allow any further increase (resulting from emissions tradability). This suggests that selection from the menu of options within the climate change regime itself could be a possibility for high-carbon-intensity developing countries.

Finally, a much larger issue relates to the sources of long-term economic dynamism. Up till now we have discussed the carbon externality as being at odds with the growth externality for high-carbon-intensity countries such as China and India. But if their future growth potential were to lie in non-energy-intensive sectors and in green technologies, these countries would need to be less concerned about preserving energy-intensive manufacturing and would be more eager to create the incentives to facilitate the necessary transition. In this case, the carbon and growth externalities would not be at odds in the policy choices but instead would be mutually reinforcing.

Given the considerable uncertainty about the optimal policy from a growth perspective, a key question is whether it is possible to devise a hedging strategy that creates incentives for technology generation and adoption in new green sectors without sacrificing the existing manufacturing sector. Many developing countries, including China, India, and

South Africa, are increasingly paying much higher prices for renewable sources of energy than for carbon-based sources. The relative price changes induced in this manner may have a less disruptive effect on downstream users of energy than an increase in carbon prices, with the government absorbing the dislocation costs that would otherwise be imposed on the private sector. Another option could involve non-price-based mechanisms such as funding R&D directly, instituting advance market commitments (see Kremer and Glennerster 2004), or through government procurement.

## 5

# Reconciling Climate Change
# and Trade Policy

[Value-added taxes are] a matter of leveling the playing field, not protectionism. And the same would be true of carbon tariffs.
—Paul Krugman, "Climate, Trade, Obama," June 29, 2009

If countries cut emissions by different amounts, or impose carbon taxes at different levels, then carbon prices are likely to differ across countries. Countries with higher carbon prices may seek to impose additional border taxes on imports from countries with lower carbon prices in order to offset the competitive disadvantage to their firms and to prevent "leakage," an increase of carbon emissions in the form of increased production in countries with lower carbon prices.

A key issue, therefore, is the scope for trade policy actions in any climate change agreement. The internationally minded U.S. senator John Kerry and the free trade–oriented senator Lindsey Graham wrote in the *New York Times:*

> We cannot sacrifice another job to competitors overseas. China and India are among the many countries investing heavily in clean-energy technologies that will produce millions of jobs. There is no reason we should surrender our marketplace to countries that do not accept environmental standards. For this reason, we should consider a border tax on items produced in countries that avoid these standards.

This is consistent with our obligations under the World Trade Organization and creates strong incentives for other countries to adopt tough environmental protections.[1]

In 2009 Senators Kerry and Barbara Boxer proposed energy reform legislation that provided for such trade actions.[2] Former president Nicolas Sarkozy of France joined the charge when he said, in September 2009, "We need to impose a carbon tax at [Europe's] borders. I will lead that battle."[3] The Nobel Prize–winning economist Paul Krugman issued his own endorsement on his *New York Times* blog. And the World Trade Organization made a guarded statement in a report issued jointly with the United Nations Environmental Program (Tamiotti and others 2009): "Rules permit, under certain conditions, the use of border tax adjustments on imported and exported products" (p. 104).

What is the likely impact of these measures? And how should they be optimally designed? These are the questions we discuss in this chapter.

The chapter is organized as follows: In the next section we describe some recent initiatives on trade actions in the context of climate change legislation and the WTO status of such actions. Then we spell out the scenarios that underlie our empirical analysis. In the following two sections we present the results of our quantitative analysis and discuss the implications of our results for the optimal design of international rules on trade actions. In the final section we present our conclusions.

## Recent Initiatives on Trade Actions and Their WTO Status

The U.S. Congress has seen recent legislative initiatives that create scope for some form of trade policy actions. The most recent bill in the Senate, introduced by Senators Kerry and Boxer in 2009, has a general provision that calls for border tax adjustments consistent with WTO provisions. This provision is not precise because the interpretation of existing WTO provisions is itself not settled. Greater specificity on border tax adjustments has been provided in a bill, the American Clean Energy and

---

1. John Kerry and Lindsey Graham, "Yes We Can (Pass Climate Change Legislation)," *New York Times,* October 10, 2009.

2. See chapter 4, n.10.

3. Peggy Hollinger, "Sarkozy Calls for Carbon Tax on Imports," *FT.com,* September 10, 2009.

Security Act (ACES), sponsored by Representatives Henry Waxman and Ed Markey and already passed by the House of Representatives, which contains two kinds of provisions with potential trade impacts.

First, ACES contemplates granting free emissions allowances to certain energy- or trade-intensive industries—likely to include iron and steel, paper and paperboard, rubber manufacturing, plastics, organic and inorganic chemicals, and petrochemicals. The amount of allowances would depend roughly on the sector's output, its carbon intensity, and the additional "tax" created by the emissions cuts. There are two ways of interpreting these allowances. It has been proposed that the allowances be related to historical output, namely, output in the previous two years, and in this case they would amount to a lump-sum transfer without any marginal impact on production decisions, and hence on trade. Alternatively, producers' knowledge that future allowances are related to current output could have an impact on current decisions on output. In this case, allowances would be closer to a production subsidy. But it is important to note that in either case the magnitude of the allowance would be related to carbon intensity in *domestic* production.

Second, the bill would require importers in certain sectors to purchase emission allowances at the going market price; eligibility criteria would be the same as for emissions allowances. This measure would be equivalent to a border tax adjustment because it would serve to raise the price of imports.[4] But the magnitude of the border tax would depend on whether the purchase of allowances must cover the actual carbon content of imports or the carbon content in comparable domestic output.[5]

---

4. Another form of border tax adjustment would be to enact an energy-performance or energy-intensity standard for certain products (say, a ton of steel cannot have a carbon footprint of more than X tons of $CO_2$) and impose that standard on both domestic and imported steel (Pauwelyn 2009).

5. This requirement on importers would kick in for imports originating in countries that are not part of a future climate change agreement or that have not signed sector-specific agreements with the United States. The requirement would become effective from 2017 and seems to be the default option unless the president intervenes to veto it. The Waxman-Markey and Kerry-Boxer bills both call for this de facto border tax provision to take into account the free emissions allowances that are granted under the provision described previously. Presumably, this is to prevent producers in selected sectors from double dipping—benefiting from the de facto subsidies under the free allowance provision *and* from the border tax adjustment on imports.

In the European Union, no clear policy initiatives have so far been taken in relation to border tax adjustments. But the former French president, Nicolas Sarkozy, called for countries in the European Union to adopt carbon taxes and to impose adjustments at the border for these taxes. In his view, the idea was now "progressing" among EU leaders "because it is more and more understood, not as a protectionist measure," but as a way to "rebalance the conditions of free-trade and competition. . . . Otherwise, it is a massive aid to relocations. We cannot tax European companies and exempt others."[6] Lord Turner, chairman of the United Kingdom's Committee on Climate Change, while noting that the distribution of free carbon permits to affected companies had for the time being addressed competitiveness concerns, has stated that border tax adjustment might be a better solution in the future. "Looking forward, we should keep an open mind about the two approaches."[7]

How do these possible trade actions align with World Trade Organization rules? WTO law and jurisprudence are evolving and are not completely clear on what types of actions would be legitimate. The legality of both the free allowances and the border tax adjustments contemplated under the recent U.S. bills is an open question (for a thoughtful examination of the legal implications of possible trade actions, see, for example, Hufbauer and others 2009; Pauwelyn 2009; Bhagwati and Mavroidis 2007; Tamiotti and others 2009).

If free emissions allowances are designed to simulate a pure transfer without any effect on marginal production decisions, they would probably not be inconsistent with WTO rules. But if they are designed to affect such marginal decisions, they could constitute a trade-distorting production subsidy. Unlike export subsidies, production subsidies per se are not prohibited by WTO rules (see part 2, "Prohibited Subsidies," of the WTO "Agreement on Subsides and Countervailing Measures" [SCM] and Pauwelyn 2009). Production subsidies are, however, actionable, including in the form of countervailing import duties by partner countries (see part 3, "Actionable Subsidies," of the WTO's "Agreement on Subsides and Countervailing Measures"). However, legitimate action

    6. See "France, Germany to Call for EU Border Tax on CO2," *EurActiv.com*, September 18, 2009.
    7. See Joshua Chaffin and Fiona Harvey, "EU Attacks Carbon Border Tax Initiative," *FT.com*, October 15, 2009.

requires the fulfillment of a number of conditions, including demonstration of injury to a domestic industry (see part 5 of the WTO's "Agreement on Subsides and Countervailing Measures").[8]

The WTO issue on border tax adjustments relates to the basic national treatment principle in article III of the 1994 General Agreement on Tariffs and Trade.[9] This article clearly permits the imposition on imports of domestic indirect taxes provided the taxes on imports are no higher than the taxes levied on comparable domestic products. Under the GATT panel ruling in the Superfund case, indirect taxes levied on domestic inputs could also be imposed on imports, provided these inputs were embodied in the final product (see Tamiotti and others 2009). However, there is no WTO jurisprudence on whether such adjustments are permissible for inputs, such as energy, that are used in production but are not themselves incorporated in the final product.[10]

Even if a border tax adjustment is permitted on inputs that are consumed but not incorporated in the final product, it is not clear whether such an adjustment should be based on the carbon content of domestic production or foreign production. The ruling in the Superfund case suggested that the border tax adjustment could be based on the amount of input embedded in the import, so there is a presumption in favor of the latter interpretation.[11] But there are important practical considerations that favor the former interpretation. For example, to implement carbon taxes based on the direct and indirect carbon content in imports would

---

8. World Trade Organization, "Agreement on Subsidies and Countervailing Measures," Geneva: World Trade Organization, n.d. (www.wto.org/english/docs_e/legal_e/24-scm_01_e.htm).

9. World Trade Organization, "WTO Analytical Index: GATT 1994, Article III" (www.wto.org/english/res_e/booksp_e/analytic_index_e/gatt1994_02_e.htm#article3).

10. Rules on export subsidies do, however, state that rebates based on energy "consumed" in the process of producing goods for export will not be deemed to be export subsidies (see World Trade Organization, "Agreement on Subsidies and Countervailing Measures," Annex I [www.wto.org/english/docs_e/legal_e/24-scm_01_e.htm]). One argument could be that it should therefore also be possible to make border tax adjustments on imports on the basis of the energy consumed in their production.

11. The discussion of the Superfund case seems to support such an interpretation: "The tax on certain imported substances equals in principle the amount of the tax which would have been imposed under the Superfund Act on the chemicals used as materials in the manufacture or production of the imported substance if these chemicals had been sold in the United States for use in the manufacture or production of the imported substance" (see World Trade Organization 1987).

require data on inputs used in their production coefficients across all sources of imports. In our empirical analysis we consider the effect of taxes that differ in their basis, that is, domestic versus foreign carbon content.[12]

## Scenarios

To compare the quantitative implications of recent initiatives, we constructed a set of scenarios, all of which involve unilateral emissions reductions by high-income countries amounting to a 17 percent cut by 2020 relative to emissions levels in 2005. This 17 percent cut is close to the unilateral cuts announced by the EU and those proposed by legislation in the United States (the Kerry-Boxer bill called for a 20 percent cut by 2020). We assume that low- and middle-income countries do not undertake any emissions reductions; modeling cuts by these countries as well is feasible but adds little to the analysis.

To depict the alternatives being considered in EU and U.S. legislation, we model four broad policy options. We abbreviate them as follows:

NBTA—No Border Tax Adjustment
BTAD—Border Tax Adjustment based on domestic carbon content
BTAF—Border Tax Adjustment based on carbon content of foreign imported goods
BTADE—Border Tax Adjustment based on domestic carbon content and applied also to exports

12. There is a another option, which would be qualitatively different from those just described, in that it would punitively target all imports from countries with lower carbon prices and would not necessarily be based on carbon content. The aim of such actions would be to attempt to change policies relating to carbon abatement across the board. These actions would be responding less to domestic trade concerns than to global environmental concerns. But this option would only be legitimate if it could be justified under the WTO's exceptions provisions in XX(b), measures necessary to protect human, animal, or plant life or health, XX(g), measures for the conservation of exhaustible natural resources (see n.12). Here we are very much in the murky waters of the WTO shrimp turtle case (see Pauwelyn 2009). WTO jurisprudence has established the permissibility of national trade policy action to protect the global environment (that is, to address cross-border externalities). However, this right entails meeting a number of conditions, including the requirement that such action be "necessary" to achieve the objective. Recent interpretations of the necessity test have required the exhaustion of other reasonable means of attaining the environmental objective—notably, international cooperation.

The first option is no border tax adjustment.

The second option, BTAD, is a border tax adjustment based on the carbon content embodied in the domestically produced good in the importing country.[13] Thus, if the United States has a $CO_2$ tax of, say, $60 per ton, and the direct and indirect $CO_2$ content in U.S. car production is 10 tons per car, the United States could apply a $CO_2$ tax of $600 (60 × 10) on the imports of cars.

The third option, BTAF, is a similar tax adjustment, except that it is based on the carbon content embodied in imports. Thus, if the direct and indirect $CO_2$ content in Indian car production is 20 tons, the United States, according to the guidelines just described, could apply a $CO_2$ tax of $1,200 on a car imported from India.[14]

A fourth option, the BTADE scenario, would be to combine a border tax adjustment on imports with a similar border tax adjustment on exports, which would relieve exporters also of the burden of paying taxes on carbon. Since export rebates would have to be based on the carbon content in domestic production, consistency would require that in this scenario the tax adjustment on imports is also based on the carbon content in domestic production.

The BTAD scenario can be seen as representing an upper bound on the trade impacts of the United States' and the EU's free emissions allowances program. As discussed earlier, this program could either have no effects on output and trade or act like a production subsidy. The BTAD scenario involves a tax on imports, which is the sum of a production subsidy and consumption tax, and will overstate the effect of the allowance program. What makes BTAD comparable with the production subsidy variant of the free allowance program is that the basis for the assistance is the carbon intensity of domestic production.

The BTAF scenario can be seen as reflecting border tax adjustment under the provision in draft U.S. legislation requiring importers to buy emissions allowances equal to the carbon content of imports, as well as under Sarkozy's proposals. Analytically, this is a border tax based on

13. Note that in all the border tax scenarios we assume that the adjustment is based on the total direct and indirect carbon content.

14. As is evident from this example, border tax adjustments based on carbon content in imports could vary with the source of imports.

how much production costs in the source (developing) country would have increased if it had imposed an identical carbon tax.

The U.S. and EU legislative initiatives do not explicitly provide for the BTADE option, which involves export rebates of carbon taxes. This probably reflects the concerns of environmentalists: it would be odd to be taking action on environmental grounds and yet exempt some part of domestic production—namely, exports—from carbon taxes. But it is important to consider this policy option. The options in BTAD and BTAF are theoretically problematic because they do not create neutral incentives between imports and exports and involve a tax on trade. As Grossman (1980) argued, neutrality in indirect taxes such as the VAT could be achieved only if border tax adjustments are symmetrical between imports and exports.

There are other possible scenarios besides the four that we examine in detail. As currently drafted, U.S. legislation provides for relief mainly for producers in energy-intensive sectors, which include chemicals, paper, ferrous metals, nonferrous metals, and mineral products. But in the four main scenarios we assume that border tax adjustments are applied on *all* merchandise imports. We do so to highlight the analytics of the various policy options and also because the application of border taxes across the board cannot be ruled out in either the United States or the EU. However, we will also discuss briefly the consequences of restricting these adjustments only to imports of energy-intensive goods, which is based on the detailed analysis in Mattoo and others (2009b).

## Quantifying the Impact of Unilateral Emissions Reduction and Trade Policy Actions

In this section we present the results of policy simulations carried out using a computable general equilibrium model.

### No Trade Policy Actions

In the benchmark scenario, which we call the NBTA (no border tax adjustment), we assume that after 2012 a carbon tax is imposed in the EU, the United States, and other industrial countries to achieve a 17 percent cut of total carbon emissions by 2020 relative to the 2005 level.

**T A B L E  5 - 1 .  Competitiveness Effects of Unilateral Emissions Reductions in Industrial Countries**

| Scenario[a] | Percent change in imports of energy-intensive manufacturing | | | Percent change in exports of energy-intensive manufacturing | | | Percent change in output of energy-intensive manufacturing | | |
|---|---|---|---|---|---|---|---|---|---|
| | High-income countries[b] | United States | EU | High-income countries | United States | EU | High-income countries | United States | EU |
| NBTA | 1.3 | 3.5 | 3.1 | −6.4 | −11.6 | −5.2 | −2.3 | −4.4 | −1.9 |
| BTAF | −16.8 | −10.1 | −38.7 | −15.7 | −15.9 | −21.5 | −0.3 | −2.5 | 1.8 |
| BTAD | −6.2 | −4.6 | −11.3 | −8.8 | −14.1 | −7.8 | −1.5 | −3.6 | −0.5 |
| BTADE | −3.2 | −1.1 | −7.8 | 1.4 | 0.7 | 4.1 | 0.0 | −0.8 | 1.0 |

Source: Mattoo and others (forthcoming).

a. NBTA: Industrial countries alone reduce emissions by 17 percent and take no trade policy action.
BTAF: Industrial countries alone reduce emissions by 17 percent and impose tariffs on all merchandise imports based on carbon content in imports.
BTAD: Industrial countries alone reduce emissions by 17 percent and impose tariffs on all merchandise imports based on carbon content in domestic production.
BTADE: Industrial countries alone reduce emissions by 17 percent with import tariffs on all merchandise imports and rebates on all merchandise exports based on carbon content in domestic production.

b. Economies are classified according to 2011 GNI per capita, calculated using the World Bank Atlas method. All countries with income $12,475 or less are classified as low and middle income, and all those with income $12,476 or more are classified as high income (for more details see http://data.worldbank.org/about/country-classifications).

We first focus on the competitiveness effects in industrial countries. The quantitative impacts are summarized in table 5-1.[15] The imposition of a carbon tax by the industrial countries can be expected to curtail domestic output of all carbon-intensive goods and services, ranging from coal, oil, and natural gas to electricity, but competitiveness effects will be felt most sharply in the case of tradable goods such as chemicals and plastics, paper products, minerals such as cement, and ferrous and non-ferrous metals. Table 5-1 shows that the impact of unilateral emissions reductions by the rich countries will lead to an increase in imports and a decline in the exports and output of the United States and the EU. For example, exports of energy-intensive manufacturing goods decline by 12 percent in the United States and 5 percent in the EU, whereas output of these goods declines by 4 percent in the United States and by 2 percent in the EU. The effects are greater in the United States than the EU because both energy and carbon intensity of these sectors in the United

15. In the text we focus on the impact on selected countries and regions (the United States, the EU, China, India, and Brazil) and selected groups (high-income and low- and middle-income). More disaggregated impacts and other data are presented in Mattoo and others (2009b, appendix tables 2–8).

**FIGURE 5-1a. Total (Direct Plus Indirect) Carbon Intensity in All Manufacturing, 2004**

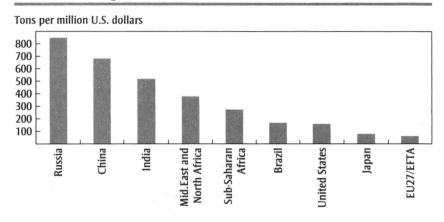

Source: Mattoo and others (forthcoming).

**FIGURE 5-1b. Total (Direct Plus Indirect) Carbon Intensity in Energy-Intensive Manufacturing, 2004**

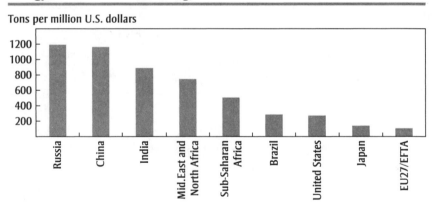

Source: Mattoo and others (forthcoming).

States is nearly double that in the EU (see figure 5-1). This also helps understand why calls for trade action at the border are more insistent in the United States than the EU.

Since developing countries do not impose comparable taxes, the action by the high-income countries leads to increased imports of carbon-intensive products from Brazil, China, and India, which therefore see an expansion in exports of these products of about 6 to 8 percent.

However, what matters for emissions is the impact on these countries' overall output and on its composition. Since exports are a small proportion of output, the increase in output of carbon-intensive sectors in Brazil, China, and India is only about 1 to 2 percent. Furthermore, this expansion pulls resources out of other sectors, which has an offsetting effect on emissions even though these other sectors are less carbon-intensive. As a result, the "leakage" effect is quite small—the emissions in low- and middle-income countries are only 1 percent higher than business-as-usual levels (see table 5-2). For example, China's emissions increase from 3,679 to 3,700 MtC (metric tons carbon) and India's from 805 to 811 MtC. Thus, given the assumptions of our model, the limited unilateral action envisaged by high-income countries to reduce their carbon emissions will not in and of itself lead to a large increase in emissions in poor countries.[16]

### Impact of Actions Based on Carbon Content in Domestic Production

Despite the limited leakage effect, we estimate that industrial countries' own energy-intensive industries are likely to face serious competitive pressures as a result of their emissions cuts. These sectors will likely put pressure on their governments to take trade policy actions, most likely in the form of additional border taxes on imports from countries that do not tax emissions at comparable levels.

BTAD involves a border tax applied on all imported products equivalent to that imposed on the carbon content in the same domestic product. The effects of such a tax on output and exports of energy-intensive sectors in the industrial countries imposing this tariff are summarized in table 5-1. The average tax across all goods is 3 to 5 percent, but the level is a little higher on energy-intensive goods, 6 to 8 percent (see table 5-3). This import tax dampens the adverse output and trade consequences of the carbon tax increase for industrial countries. For example, imports of energy-intensive goods now decline by 4.6 percent in the United States, compared to a 3.5 percent increase without import action, and output of such goods declines by 3.6 percent compared with a 4.4 percent decline without offsetting trade action (see table 5-1).

16. This result, like all others, is conditional on the supply and demand elasticities of our computable general equilibrium (CGE) model. For a comparison of our results with those of other models, see Mattoo and others (2009b, pp. 33–35, "Unilateral Action and Leakage").

**TABLE 5-2. Impact on Emissions Reductions in Alternative Scenarios**

| Scenario[a] | World total | High-income countries[b] | United States | EU | Low- and middle-income countries[b] | China | Brazil | India | Sub-Saharan Africa |
|---|---|---|---|---|---|---|---|---|---|
| Percent change in emissions relative to business-as-usual in 2020 | | | | | | | | | |
| NBTA | −9.3 | −28.4 | −33.5 | −30.0 | 1.0 | 0.6 | 1.3 | 0.8 | 3.0 |
| BTAF | −10.9 | −28.5 | −33.5 | −30.0 | −1.5 | −1.7 | 0.6 | −1.6 | 0.7 |
| BTAD | −9.8 | −28.4 | −33.5 | −30.0 | 0.3 | 0.0 | 0.8 | 0.3 | 2.3 |
| BTADE | −10.0 | −28.5 | −33.5 | −30.0 | 0.0 | −0.3 | 0.8 | −0.2 | 2.2 |
| Percent change in emissions relative to 2005 | | | | | | | | | |
| NBTA17 | 56.9 | −11.4 | −17.0 | −17.0 | 122.5 | 183.5 | 37.6 | 156.5 | 82.5 |
| BTAF | 54.1 | −11.6 | −17.0 | −17.0 | 117.2 | 177.0 | 36.6 | 150.3 | 78.4 |
| BTAD | 56.2 | −11.5 | −17.0 | −17.0 | 121.1 | 182.0 | 36.8 | 155.0 | 81.4 |
| BTADE | 55.8 | −11.5 | −17.0 | −17.0 | 120.4 | 181.2 | 36.8 | 153.7 | 81.1 |

Source: Mattoo and others (forthcoming).

a. NBTA17: Industrial countries alone reduce emissions by 17 percent and take no trade policy action.

BTAF: Industrial countries alone reduce emissions by 17 percent and impose tariffs on all merchandise imports based on carbon content in imports.

BTAD: Industrial countries alone reduce emissions by 17 percent and impose tariffs on all merchandise imports based on carbon content in domestic production.

BTADE: Industrial countries alone reduce emissions by 17 percent with import tariffs on all merchandise imports and rebates on all merchandise exports based on carbon content in domestic production.

b. See table 5-1.

**TABLE 5-3. Additional Tariff on Exports, by Country of Origin**
Percent

| Country of origin | BTAF[a] | | BTAD[a] | | BTADE[a] | | | |
|---|---|---|---|---|---|---|---|---|
| | | | | | Tariff | | Export rebate | |
| | All manufacturing | Energy-intensive manufacturing | All manufacturing | Energy-intensive manufacturing | All manufacturing | Energy-intensive manufacturing | All manufacturing | Energy-intensive manufacturing |
| Rest of high-income countries | 5.1 | 8.7 | 3.2 | 5.8 | 3.3 | 6.1 | 4.0 | 6.8 |
| Brazil | 5.8 | 9.9 | 4.4 | 7.1 | 4.5 | 7.4 | 4.3 | 6.7 |
| China | 26.1 | 42.7 | 3.1 | 6.2 | 3.3 | 6.5 | 3.7 | 6.8 |
| India | 20.3 | 28.5 | 3.5 | 6.8 | 3.6 | 7.0 | 7.1 | 9.8 |
| Russia | 35.3 | 40.0 | 5.2 | 6.5 | 5.4 | 6.7 | 3.5 | 5.1 |
| Rest of East Asia | 9.5 | 14.8 | 3.1 | 5.7 | 3.2 | 6.0 | 3.8 | 7.0 |
| Rest of South Asia | 10.3 | 39.2 | 3.0 | 5.7 | 3.1 | 5.9 | 3.8 | 6.4 |
| Rest of Eastern Europe and Central Asia | 23.5 | 39.7 | 4.1 | 6.7 | 4.2 | 6.9 | 3.7 | 5.5 |
| Middle East and North Africa | 16.6 | 30.4 | 3.2 | 6.3 | 3.3 | 6.5 | 4.0 | 6.3 |
| Sub-Saharan Africa | 10.9 | 19.0 | 3.9 | 6.6 | 4.1 | 6.8 | 3.7 | 6.4 |
| Rest of Latin America | 6.6 | 11.8 | 4.2 | 7.6 | 4.4 | 8.0 | 4.7 | 7.7 |

Source: Mattoo and others (forthcoming).

a. BTAF: Industrial countries alone reduce emissions by 17 percent and impose tariffs on all merchandise imports based on carbon content in imports.

BTAD: Industrial countries alone reduce emissions by 17 percent and impose tariffs on all merchandise imports based on carbon content in domestic production.

BTADE: Industrial countries alone reduce emissions by 17 percent with import tariffs on all merchandise imports and rebates on all merchandise exports based on carbon content in domestic production.

The impact on all major countries in the BTAD scenario is summarized in table 5-4. Changes in welfare and output of low- and middle-income countries are less than 1 percent, and exports decline by around 3 percent. The increase in developing-country emissions as a result of this action is 0.3 percent as compared with 1 percent without trade action, so that global emissions also decline a little more, 9.8 percent, as compared to 9.3 percent without trade action.[17]

### Impact of Actions Based on Carbon Content in Imports

Trade action involving border tax adjustments based on the carbon content in imports and applied to all manufacturing sectors (BTAF) would address both competitiveness and environmental concerns in industrial countries, but it would be more disruptive for developing-country exporters of manufactured goods. Manufacturing output in energy-intensive industries in the United States would now decline by only 2.5 percent, and in the EU it would actually increase by 1.8 percent. Currently these effects are not concentrated only in energy-intensive manufacturing but are spread out over the entire manufacturing sector. As a result, the effects on aggregate manufacturing in high-income countries are positive, resulting in an increase in output. Under this scenario, low- and middle-income countries' emissions would also decline by 1.5 percent as against the negligible impact (0.3 percent increase) when actions are based on the carbon content of domestic production.

These outcomes in the high-income countries would come at a huge cost for developing-country trading partners such as China and India. Since production in these countries is much more carbon-intensive than in OECD countries, import taxes on all manufactured goods in the BTAF scenario are much higher than in the BTAD scenario. The average tariff on manufactured goods imports from China would be about 26 percent and from India, about 20 percent (see table 5-3).[18]

---

17. Note that if high-income countries allocated free emissions allowances along the lines discussed in the section "Recent Initiatives on Trade Actions and Their WTO Status," the impact on emissions reductions would be smaller than if they imposed a tariff.

18. Production could be relatively carbon-intensive in developing countries for these broad GTAP (Global Trade Analysis Project) categories, both because individual products are produced more carbon-intensively and because the broad product categories include more carbon-intensive products.

**TABLE 5-4. Impact on Welfare, Manufacturing Output, and Exports**

| Scenario[a] | World total | High-income countries | United States | EU | Low- and middle-income countries | China | India | Brazil | Sub-Saharan Africa |
|---|---|---|---|---|---|---|---|---|---|
| Percent change in welfare | | | | | | | | | |
| NBTA | -0.5 | -0.6 | -0.6 | -0.7 | -0.3 | -0.2 | 0.0 | -0.1 | -0.5 |
| BTAF | -1.0 | -0.4 | -0.4 | -0.4 | -2.4 | -3.7 | -1.4 | -0.5 | -1.2 |
| BTAD | -0.6 | -0.5 | -0.5 | -0.5 | -0.8 | -0.6 | -0.3 | -0.4 | -1.0 |
| BTADE | -0.5 | -0.5 | -0.6 | -0.5 | -0.5 | -0.3 | 0.1 | -0.3 | -0.7 |
| Percent change in output of total manufacturing | | | | | | | | | |
| NBTA17 | -0.4 | -0.8 | -1.2 | -0.8 | 0.1 | -0.2 | 0.1 | 0.4 | 0.8 |
| BTAF | -0.8 | 0.8 | -0.2 | 1.9 | -3.0 | -3.6 | -3.3 | 1.5 | -0.9 |
| BTAD | -0.5 | -0.6 | -1.2 | -0.3 | -0.4 | -0.5 | -0.4 | 0.3 | 0.4 |
| BTADE | -0.4 | -0.3 | -0.5 | 0.0 | -0.6 | -0.5 | -0.5 | 0.0 | -0.1 |
| Percent change in exports of total manufacturing | | | | | | | | | |
| NBTA17 | -1.0 | -1.8 | -2.3 | -2.1 | -0.1 | -0.9 | -0.3 | 1.0 | 2.7 |
| BTAF | -12.9 | -11.3 | -10.1 | -23.2 | -14.8 | -20.8 | -16.0 | 1.9 | -8.8 |
| BTAD | -4.0 | -4.8 | -6.5 | -6.6 | -3.2 | -3.4 | -3.2 | -2.5 | -1.8 |
| BTADE | -1.2 | -0.5 | 0.0 | 0.5 | -2.0 | -1.8 | -2.1 | -0.6 | -2.0 |

Source: Mattoo and others (forthcoming).

a. NBTA: Industrial countries alone reduce emissions by 17 percent and take no trade policy action.
BTAF: Industrial countries alone reduce emissions by 17 percent and impose tariffs on all merchandise imports based on carbon content in imports.
BTAD: Industrial countries alone reduce emissions by 17 percent and impose tariffs on all merchandise imports based on carbon content in domestic production.
BTADE: Industrial countries alone reduce emissions by 17 percent with import tariffs on all merchandise imports and rebates on all merchandise exports based on carbon content in domestic production.

As a result, China's aggregate manufacturing exports decline by about 21 percent and India's, by 16 percent. In both countries, manufacturing output declines by close to 3.5 percent (see table 5-4). Brazil is much less affected because its exports are far less carbon-intensive.

The impact on welfare is also significant: the BTAD scenario would have smaller welfare effects in China, India, and all low- and middle-income countries, whereas the BTAF scenario would reduce welfare in these countries by 3.7 (China), 1.4 (India), and 2.4 (all low- and middle-income countries percent (see table 5-4).

Thus, trade policy actions based on the carbon content of imports applied to all imports would have substantial effects.

### Impact of Actions Based on Carbon Content in Domestic Production but Applied to Imports and Exports

Recall that border tax adjustments in the BTAD scenario are akin to a tariff on imports. Trade theory suggests that a tax on imports is also a tax on exports, and so this type of adjustment taxes trade twice and is likely to be inefficient. The way to eliminate the distortion would be to have symmetrical tax adjustments so that the indirect tax burden on exports is also relieved (see Grossman 1980; Lockwood and Whalley 2008). We call this the efficient border tax (BTADE).

Border taxes on imports and exports will allay the competitiveness concerns in industrial countries to a greater degree than the corresponding tax adjustment applied only to imports, because these countries' exporters' competitiveness is also improved. Thus, energy-intensive manufacturing sectors in the United States witness a decline in output of 0.8 percent under BTADE compared with 3.6 percent in BTAD. In the EU, BTADE actually allows a more than full clawback of competitiveness losses for energy-intensive producers because output increases by 1 percent compared with a 0.5 percent decline in the BTAD scenario.[19]

The impact on developing-country trade is also clearly smaller under BTADE than under BTAD (and of course it is much smaller than under the BTAF scenario). For example, manufacturing exports of China and India decline by 1.8 percent and 2.1 percent, respectively, in the BTADE scenario, compared with 3.4 and 3.2 percent, respectively, in the BTAD

19. In fact, efficient border tax adjustment (BTADE) addresses the competitiveness concerns of the energy-intensive sectors in some high-income countries such as the United States even more effectively than the drastic action in the BTAF scenario, because the output benefits of export rebates are greater than of further increases in tariffs.

scenario. This seems to be in accordance with the Grossman (1980) result that the BTAD border adjustment taxes trade and hence shrinks trading opportunities also for partner countries.[20]

A symmetrical border tax adjustment would also be superior to the alternatives (BTAF and BTAD) from a global efficiency perspective. We know that trade actions based on carbon content in imports imply a very high tariff and hence lead to large global efficiency losses of 1 percent. Under BTADE and BTAD, welfare declines are nearly halved, with BTADE being superior to BTAD. Global welfare declines by 0.52 percent in the former and by 0.58 percent in the latter. Global emissions also decline marginally more in the BTADE scenario (10 percent) than in the BTAD scenario (9.8 percent).[21]

The foregoing discussion suggests that from the perspectives of political economy in industrial countries, of trade interests of developing countries, and of global efficiency, the symmetrical and efficient border tax adjustment scenario (BTADE) is the least undesirable alternative.

### Impact of Border Taxes Applied to Energy-Intensive Imports

We have examined the impacts of trade actions applied to all merchandise imports. What if they are only applied to energy-intensive imports? It turns out that if border taxes were applied only to energy-intensive imports, they would broadly achieve the goals of minimizing the adverse competitiveness effects in industrial countries from unilateral emissions reductions while also moderating the trade impact on developing-country partners. For example, the decline in output of energy-intensive manufacturing in the United States in these scenarios is 2.6 percent if tariffs are based on domestic carbon content, the BTADR scenario, and 0.5 percent if tariffs are based on foreign carbon content, the BTAFR scenario (see Mattoo and others 2009b). In both BTAD and BTADE, the decline in China's and India's manufacturing exports is 1 to 3 percent.

---

20. However, the BTADE scenario is not superior to the BTAD scenario for developing countries' manufacturing output.

21. Another way of understanding the BTADE scenario is as a consumption tax on emissions, and the no border tax adjustment scenario (NBTA), as a pure production tax on emissions. Global welfare decline is marginally lower in the NBTA scenario (0.49 percent) than in the BTADE scenario (0.52 percent), but the emissions decline is greater in the BTADE scenario (10 percent) than in the BTAD scenario (9.3 percent). Thus, a pure consumption-based tax is overwhelmingly superior to a tax that distorts trade (BTAD) but is not unambiguously superior to a pure production tax.

Despite these results, limiting the scope of trade actions to energy-intensive products would have problems, which we discuss in the next section.[22]

## Implications for International Trade Rules

The best outcome from a purely trade perspective would be to have no scope for carbon-based border tax adjustment—but, obviously, not from an environmental perspective. That is why, as we noted at the beginning of this chapter, unconstrained border tax adjustments are already under consideration and enjoy a certain measure of support, including from the WTO. It may, therefore, be useful to assess alternatives, from both trade and environmental perspectives.

It is worth recalling the alternative rationales for border tax adjustments. From a *trade perspective,* border tax adjustments applied symmetrically to imports and exports essentially transform production-based taxes into consumption-based taxes (Grossman 1980). Such adjustments do not alter the incentives within a country to produce exports or importables. From an *environmental perspective,* border tax adjustments are aimed at ensuring that the emissions reductions achieved within a country through a tax (production tax) are not totally offset by the increase in emissions that occurs in partner countries by virtue of expanded trade. That is, border tax adjustments attempt to tax the emissions in trade. One difference between the efficiency and environmental motivations for BTAs is that with the former, a country would apply BTAs regardless of what partner countries do. With the latter, in contrast, BTAs are typically aimed only at countries that do not take some or comparable action on emissions reductions.

What would be the status of different forms of BTAs under existing trade rules? Current WTO rules and jurisprudence are not settled. If taxes on consumed inputs cannot be subject to border tax adjustment, then it would seem that neither taxes based on the carbon content of domestic production nor those based on the carbon content embodied in imports can be the basis for border adjustments. Of course, both bases for applying border taxes could be justified by the environmental

---

22. Mattoo and others (forthcoming) show that these results are robust to alternative emissions reductions by high-income countries.

exceptions provisions of Article XX of the 1994 GATT, but that avenue itself is untested and uncertain.[23] If indirect taxes on inputs such as carbon and energy that are consumed in production can be subject to border tax adjustment—which is far from clear—then the presumption would seem to be that these taxes would be based on the carbon content embodied in imports. This interpretation is suggested by the GATT dispute settlement panel's ruling in the Superfund case, and indeed, it would be consistent with viewing border tax adjustments as environmental measures aimed at taxing the consumption of the offending input.[24]

Our results suggest that BTAs based on carbon content in imports would have drastic trade consequences. There is also a serious practical problem with BTAs based on inputs that are consumed in the process of producing the output. Implementing carbon taxes based on the direct and indirect carbon content in imports would require data not only on production methods in all source countries but also information on the origin of each input. Different imports from one country could have different carbon content depending on where the inputs used in production were sourced: U.S. imports of car A from Malaysia that used steel from, say, Brazil would face a different kind of border tax adjustment than car B, also from Malaysia, that used steel from China. In a world of internationally fragmented production, establishing the precise carbon content of any particular product would be nearly impossible. These daunting informational requirements could allow considerable scope for rent-seeking behavior as firms try to manipulate information to influence the taxes imposed on particular goods from particular countries.

These considerations suggest that a possible compromise between no border tax adjustments, which is best from a trade perspective, and adjustment based on carbon content of imports (BTAF), which is attractive from an environmental perspective, could be adjustment based on the carbon content in domestic production (BTAD or BTADE). Countries could accept this principle as a pragmatic and negotiated compromise not just between trade and environmental concerns but also between the interests of different countries. The case for such adjustment is strengthened by our finding that unilateral emissions reductions

23. See n.12.
24. World Trade Organization (1987).

by industrial countries lead primarily to a loss in industrial competitiveness rather than to significant "leakage" of emissions. Adjustment based on carbon content in domestic production addresses competitiveness concerns in industrial countries without inflicting undue pain on developing countries.

Could the suggested application of uniform BTA across countries be seen as discrimination against those such as Brazil whose production is relatively less carbon-intensive? Although this concern is valid in principle, in practice it could be less important. Even developing countries such as Brazil have a higher carbon intensity of production than the industrial countries, so any uniform BTA would not penalize them unduly in absolute terms, even though it would not take into account Brazil's low carbon intensity relative to, say, China. Furthermore, an importing country such as the United States could choose to exempt from BTAs countries such as those in the EU that either were very carbon-efficient or were taking action to reduce emissions. In fact, U.S. legislation is pointing in this direction.

One other issue relates to the choice between border tax adjustments applied symmetrically to imports and exports (BTADE) and those applied only to imports (BTAD). From a trade perspective, the former is superior. Our interesting result is that even from an emissions perspective, the symmetrical adjustment is superior. But it is possible that environmentalists will object to rebating energy taxes on inputs that go into export production. Whether countries adopt the symmetrical version (BTADE) or the imports-only variant (BTAD) is something that could best be left to individual countries to decide on the basis of their respective weighting of the trade and environmental concerns.

How would our proposed approach compare with other proposals? Consider first the arguments made by Paul Krugman: "The WTO has looked at the issue, and suggests that carbon tariffs may be viewed the same way as border adjustments associated with value-added taxes. It has long been accepted that a VAT is essentially a sales tax—a tax on consumers—which for administrative reasons is collected from producers. Because it's essentially a tax on consumers, it's legal, and *also economically efficient,* to collect it on imported goods as well as domestic production; it's a matter of leveling the playing field, not protectionism. And the same would be true of carbon tariffs" (emphasis added).[25]

25. Krugman (2009).

But it should be emphasized that border tax adjustments applied to imports alone and not to exports would not be "economically efficient" because they would distort trade. As we suggest, there may be good environmental reasons to limit trade actions to imports alone, but there is then a conflict with allocative efficiency that must be recognized.

Our proposed approach would be slightly different from one hybrid system for border tax adjustments that has been widely cited. Hufbauer and others (2009) propose that there would be no border tax adjustments on imports from a country that was taking substantial action on emissions reductions or reductions comparable to those of the importing country. They would, however, allow a country to apply a border tax adjustment on imports if the domestic emissions tax in the importing country is greater than in the exporting country, reflecting the destination principle. As noted, this amounts to distorting trade. While these authors do not specify whether the border tax adjustment on imports would be based on the carbon content of imports or domestic production, the spirit of their proposal seems to strongly favor the former. Thus, their proposal differs from ours in two ways: they would not allow for symmetrical border tax adjustments (BTADE) and they would in principle allow and even require border tax adjustments based on the carbon content in imports (BTAF). We have shown that the BTAF option would have serious trade consequences, and even a more restricted application of border tax adjustments is problematic, as we argue later.

What about the alternative of limiting the scope for trade actions to energy-intensive imports, which our results suggest would, from a trade perspective, be close to the symmetrical border tax adjustment? There are a number of problems with this approach. First, it would still leave room for border taxes based on the carbon content of imports with the attendant problems discussed earlier. Second, even if trade actions were initially restricted to energy-intensive goods, they could provoke demands for extension: non-energy-intensive sectors would ask why they were being excluded from import relief, especially given that there are large cross-country differences in total carbon intensity even in non-energy-intensive sectors (Mattoo and others 2009b). The risk that rules to restrict trade action to selected sectors could be open to future extension is suggested by a recent Council of the European Union decision on border tax adjustments.[26]

26. Council of the European Union (2009).

Indeed any border tax adjustment option is vulnerable to the slippery-slope phenomenon. If the principle is accepted that border tax adjustments could be applied to nonembodied inputs, such as energy, that are consumed in the process of production, then this might open the door to similar adjustments for taxes on other inputs that are not embodied, and perhaps to other domestic taxes and regulations more broadly. This is another argument for disallowing the principle of carbon-based border tax adjustments in the first place.

Finally, one way of ruling out border tax adjustments by industrial countries would be for developing countries to impose export taxes on carbon-intensive goods. This would have a number of advantages for developing countries. Since such an action would address both competitiveness and environmental concerns in industrial countries, it would head off the pressure for BTAs in these countries. Developing countries would get to keep the tax revenues for themselves whereas with a BTA the importing country would obtain the revenues. The analogy here is with a voluntary export restraint compared to an import restriction. Developing countries could also calibrate the cost shock that they would impose on their exporters more appropriately than could an importing country imposing a BTA. For example, in the BTAF scenario, exports from China face an unfavorable cost shock in the form of a U.S. emissions tax based on Chinese carbon intensity. China could impose a lower export tax than the U.S. emissions tax. Any such export tax option would obviously have to be negotiated between importing and exporting countries bilaterally or multilaterally, and its attractiveness would depend on the likely alternatives.

## Conclusions

If the major industrial countries make emissions reductions of the magnitude currently proposed, their industries will clamor to offset the competitiveness pressure of imports from countries that make less ambitious reductions. If, say, industrial countries reduce emissions by 17 percent by 2020 relative to 2005 levels, energy-intensive industries in the United States will face output declines of around 4 percent. (There will also be demands from environmentalists for trade action to prevent emissions "leakage," but our estimates show that these concerns are not warranted.)

Industrial countries can respond to competitiveness concerns by imposing tariffs or border tax adjustments. The most extreme form of trade action would be one that is based on the carbon content of imports and applied to all merchandise imports. This would no doubt address the competitiveness and environmental concerns in high-income countries but would come at the price of seriously damaging the trade prospects of developing-country trading partners. Such an action would imply average tariffs on merchandise imports from India and China of over 20 percent and would depress manufacturing exports between 16 and 21 percent.

A border tax adjustment based on the carbon content in domestic production would broadly address the competitiveness concerns of producers in high-income countries while inflicting less damage on developing-country trade. So this option is the least undesirable from a developing-country trade perspective. This suggests that as part of any international agreement on climate change, all countries could seek to negotiate rules in the WTO that would either prohibit all forms of carbon-based border tax adjustment or would allow under the strictest conditions the least undesirable option. Whether a domestic carbon-based tax should be applied symmetrically to imports and exports or only to imports is a choice that could be left to individual countries in accordance with their relative assessment of trade and environmental concerns.

International agreement on trade actions should be pursued as part of an international agreement on climate change rather than left to future separate negotiations by the WTO. Otherwise developing countries will remain vulnerable to trade policy action, especially an extreme version of it. This would render uncertain the overall benefits to developing countries of international cooperation on climate change, which might introduce more tensions into the international atmosphere and worsen the prospects for achieving such cooperation.

# References

Agarwal, Anil, and Sunita Narain. 1991. *Global Warming in an Unequal World: A Case of Environmental Colonialism*. New Delhi: Centre for Science and Environment.

Antholis, William. 2009. "India and Climate Change." *Wall Street Journal*, July 20.

Baer, Paul, Tom Athanasiou, and Sivan Kartha. 2007. "The Greenhouse Development Rights Framework: The Right to Development in a Climate Constrained World." Publication Series on Ecology, volume 1. Berlin: Heinrich Böll Foundation, Christian Aid, EcoEquity, and Stockholm Environment Institute (November).

Barro, Robert J., and Xavier Sala-i-Martin. 2005. *Economic Growth*. MIT Press.

Berndt, Ernst R., Rachel Glennerster, Michael R. Kremer, Jean Lee, Ruth Levine, Georg Weizsäcker, and Heidi Williams. 2007. "Advance Market Commitments for Vaccines Against Neglected Diseases: Estimating Costs and Effectiveness." *Health Economics* 16, no. 3: 491–511.

Bhagwati, Jagdish. 2009a. "Reflections on Climate Change and Trade." In *Climate Change, Trade, and Competitiveness: Is a Collision Inevitable?* edited by Isaac Sorkin and Lael Brainard. Brookings.

———. 2009b. "Agreeing on a Framework Agreement at Copenhagen." *Australian Financial Review*, December 9.

Bhagwati, Jagdish, and Petros C. Mavroidis. 2007. "Is Action Against US Exports for Failure to Sign the Kyoto Protocol WTO-Legal?" *World Trade Review* 6, no. 2: 299–310.

Birdsall, Nancy, and Arvind Subramanian. 2009. "Energy Needs and Efficiency, Not Emissions: Re-framing the Climate Change Narrative." CGD Working Paper 187. Washington: Center for Global Development (November).

Bosetti, Valentine, and J. Frankel. 2009. "Global Climate Policy Architecture and Political Feasibility: Specific Formulas and Emission Targets to Attain 460 PPM CO2 Concentrations." Discussion Paper 09-30. Harvard University, Kennedy School of Government, Belfer Center for Science and International Affairs, Harvard Project on Climate Agreements.

Brautigam, Deborah, and Stephen Knack. 2004. "Foreign Aid, Institutions and Governance in Sub-Saharan Africa." *Economic Development and Cultural Change* 52, no. 2: 255–86.

Cao, Jing. 2008. "Reconciling Human Development and Climate Protection: Perspectives from Developing Countries on Post-2012 International Climate Change Policy." Discussion Paper 08-25. Harvard University, Kennedy School of Government, Belfer Center for Science and International Affairs, Harvard Project on International Climate Agreements.

Caselli, Francesco. 2004. "Accounting for Cross-Country Income Differences." CEPR Discussion Paper no. 4703. London: Centre for Economic Policy Research, October.

Chakravarty, Shoibal, Ananth Chikkatur, Heleen de Coninck, Stephen Pacala, Robert Socolow, and Massimo Tavoni. 2009. "Sharing Global CO2 Emission Reductions among One Billion High Emitters." *Proceedings of the National Academy of Sciences of the United States of America* 26, no. 29: 11884–88.

Cline, William R. 2007. "Global Warming and Agriculture: Impact Estimates by Country." Washington: Center for Global Development and Peterson Institute for International Economics.

Collier, Paul. 2007. *The Bottom Billion: Why the Poorest Countries Are Failing and What Can Be Done About It.* Oxford University Press.

Cooper, Richard N. 2008. "The Case for Charges on Greenhouse Gas Emissions." Harvard University, Kennedy School of Government, Belfer Center for Science and International Affairs, Harvard Project on International Climate Agreements (October).

Council of the European Union. 2009. "Council Conclusions on the Further Development of the EU Position on a Comprehensive Post-2012 Climate Agreement (Contribution of the Spring European Council)." Brussels: March 2 (www.consilium. europa.eu/uedocs/cms_data/docs/pressdata/en/envir/106429.pdf).

Davis, Steven J., and Ken Caldeira. 2010. "Consumption-Based Accounting of CO2 Emissions." PNAS Early Edition, March 8 (www.pnas.org/content/early/2010/ 02/23/0906974107.full.pdf+html).

Dietz, Simon, Cameron Hepburn, and Nicholas Stern. 2007. "Economics, Ethics, and Climate Change." Paper. Social Science Research Network (http://papers.ssrn.com/ sol3/papers.cfm?abstract_id=1090572).

Dixit, Avinash. 2009. "Governance Institutions and Economic Activity." *American Economic Review* 99, no. 1: 5–24.

Djankov, Simeon, Jose G. Montalvo, and Marta Reynal-Querol. 2005. "The Curse of Aid." Washington: World Bank.

Dubash, Navroz K. 2009a. "Toward a Progressive Indian and Global Climate Politics." CPR Climate Initiative Working Paper 2009/1. New Delhi: Centre for Policy Research Climate Initiative (September).

———. 2009b. "Climate Change through a Development Lens." Development and Change Background Paper. World Development Report 2010. New Delhi: Jawaharlal Nehru University.

Easterly, William. 2007. *The White Man's Burden: Why the West's Efforts to Aid the Rest Have Done So Much Ill and So Little Good.* New York: Penguin.

Easterly, William, Ross Levine, and David Roodman. 2004. "Aid, Policies, and Growth: Comment." *American Economic Review* 94, no. 3: 774–80.

Elbadawi, Ibrahim. 1999. "External Aid: Help or Hindrance to Export Orientation in Africa." *Journal of African Economies* 8, no. 4: 578–616.

Ferguson, Niall, and Moritz Schularick. 2007. " 'Chimerica' and the Global Asset Market Boom." *International Finance* 10, no. 3: 215–39.

Frankel, Jeffrey. 2007. "Formulas for Quantitative Emission Targets." Faculty Research Working Paper Series RWP07-011. Harvard University.

German Advisory Council on Global Change. 2009. "Limiting Global Warming to 2° Centigrade." Chapter 2 in "Solving the Climate Dilemma: The Budget Approach." Special report. Berlin: German Advisory Council on Global Change (WBGU).

German Agency for Technical Cooperation, Climate Protection Program. 2004. "South-North Dialogue on Equity in the Greenhouse. A Proposal for an Adequate and Equitable Global Climate Agreement." Eschborn, Germany: German Agency for Technical Cooperation (GTZ).

Ghosh, Prodipto. 2009. "National Action Plan on Climate Change." Report prepared for Prime Minister's Council on Climate Change. New Delhi: October (http://moef. nic.in/downloads/home/Pg01-52.pdf).

———. 2010. "Climate Change Debate: The Story from India." In *Dealing with Climate Change: Setting a Global Agenda for Mitigation and Adaptation,* edited by R. K. Pauchuri. New Delhi: Energy and Resources Institute.

Gourinchas, Pierre-Olivier, and Olivier Jeanne. 2007. "Capital Flows to Developing Countries: The Allocation Puzzle." NBER Working Paper 13602. Cambridge, Mass.: National Bureau of Economic Research.

Government of Brazil. 1997. "Paper No. 1: Brazil—Proposed Elements to the United Nations Framework Convention on Climate Change, Presented by Brazil in Response to the Berlin Mandate." In "Implementation of the Berlin Mandate: Additional Proposals from Parties," by the United Nations Framework Convention on Climate Change, Ad Hoc Group on the Berlin Mandate (http://unfccc.int/cop4/resource/docs/1997/agbm/misc01a3.htm).

Government of India, Ministry of Environment and Forests. 2009. "India: Taking on Climate Change: Twenty Recent Initiatives Related to Climate Change." New Delhi: September (http://moef.nic.in/downloads/home/twenty-CC-initiatives.pdf).

Grossman, Gene. 1980. "Border Tax Adjustments: Do They Distort Trade?" *Journal of International Economics* 10, no. 1 (February): 117–28.

Houser, Trevor. 2010. "Copenhagen, the Accord, and the Way Forward." PIIE Policy Brief No. 10-5. Washington: Peterson Institute for International Economics.

Hufbauer, Gary Clyde, Steve Charnovitz, and Jisun Kim. 2009. "Global Warming and the World Trading System." Washington: Peterson Institute for International Economics.

International Energy Agency. 2009. "How The Energy Sector Can Deliver on a Climate Agreement in Copenhagen: Special Early Excerpt of the World Energy Outlook for the Bangkok UNFCCC Meeting." Paris: International Energy Agency and Organization for Economic Cooperation and Development (www.frankhaugwitz. info/doks/cdm/2009_10_IEA_climate_change_excerpt_China.pdf).

Jacoby, Henry D., Mustafa H. Babiker, Sergey Paltsev, and John M. Reilly. 2008. "Sharing the Burden of GHG Reductions." Report no. 167. Massachusetts Institute of Technology, Joint Program on the Science and Policy of Global Change.

Jones, Benjamin, and Ben Olken. 2008. "The Anatomy of Start-Stop Growth." *Review of Economics and Statistics* 90, no. 1 (May): 582–87.

Joshi, Vijay. 2009. "Comments on Climate Change and India: Implications and Policy Options." *India Policy Forum 2009–10,* volume 6: 129–33 (http://www.ncaer.org/downloads/Journals/IPF_2009_10_IPF-Vol_6.pdf).

Joshi, Vijay, and Urjit Patel. 2009. "India and a Carbon Deal." *Economic & Political Weekly* 44, no. 31: 71–78.

Kanitkar, Tejal, T. Jayaraman, Mario D'Souza, Mukul Sanwal, Prabir Purkayastha, and Rajbans Talwar. 2010. "Global Carbon Space, Emissions, Trajectories, and Burden Sharing in Mitigation Actions." Paper presented at CASS Forum on Climate Justice and the Carbon Budget Approach, Beijing, April 15–16.

Knack, Stephen. 2001. "Aid Dependence and the Quality of Governance: Cross-Country Empirical Tests." *Southern Economic Journal* 68, no. 2 (October): 310–29.

Kremer, Michael, and Rachel Glennerster. 2004. *Strong Medicine: Creating Incentives for Pharmaceutical Research on Neglected Diseases.* Princeton University Press.

Krugman, Paul. 2009. "Climate, Trade, Obama." *The Conscience of a Liberal* (blog), January 29.

Lockwood, Ben, and John Whalley. 2008. "Carbon Motivated Border Tax Adjustments: Old Wine in Green Bottles?" NBER Working Paper 14025. Cambridge, Mass.: National Bureau of Economic Research.

Mattoo, Aaditya, and Arvind Subramanian. 2012. "Equity in Climate Change: An Analytical Review." *World Development* 40, no. 6.

Mattoo, Aaditya, Arvind Subramanian, Dominique van der Mensbrugghe, and Jianwu He. 2009a. "Can Global De-Carbonization Inhibit Developing Country Industrialization?" Policy Research Working Paper 5121. Washington: World Bank, Development Research Group, Trade and Integration Team (November).

———. 2009b. "Reconciling Climate Change and Trade Policy." Policy Research Working Paper No. 5123. Washington: World Bank, Development Research Group, Trade and Integration Team (November).

———. 2012. "Can Global De-Carbonization Inhibit Developing Country Industrialization?" *World Bank Economic Review* 26: 296–319.

———. Forthcoming. "Trade Effects of Alternative Carbon Border-Tax Schemes." *Review of World Economics.*

Meyer, A. 2000. *Contraction and Convergence: The Global Solution to Climate Change.* Green Books: London.

Moyo, Dambisa. 2009. *Dead Aid: Why Aid Is Not Working and How There Is Another Way for Africa.* New York: Farrar, Straus and Giroux.

Müller, Benito, Niklas Höhne, and Christian Ellermann. 2007. "Differentiating (Historic) Responsibilities for Climate Change: Summary Report." Paper presented at the twenty-seventh session of the Subsidiary Body for Scientific and Technological Advice (SBSTA) of the UN Framework Convention on Climate Change, Bali, December 3–11 (www.oxfordclimatepolicy.org/publications/documents/Differen tiatingResponsibility.pdf).

Nordhaus, William D. 2011. "Estimates of the Social Cost of Carbon: Background and Results from the RICE-2011 Model." Cowles Foundation Discussion Paper 1826. Yale University, Cowles Foundation for Research on Economics (October).

———. 2007. "The Challenge of Global Warming: Economic Models and Environmental Policy in the DICE-2007 Model." Unpublished manuscript (http://nordhaus.econ.yale.edu/dice_mss_072407_all.pdf).

Pan, Jiahua, Ying Chen, Wenjun Wang, and Chenxi Li. 2008. "Carbon Budget Proposal: Global Emissions under Carbon Budget Constraint on an Individual Basis for an Equitable and Sustainable Post 2012 International Climate Regime." Beijing: Chinese Academy of Social Sciences, Research Centre for Sustainable Development.

Pan, Jiahua, J. Phillips, and Y. Chen. 2008. "China's Balance of Emissions Embodied in Trade: Approaches to Measurement and Allocating International Responsibility." *Oxford Review of Economic Policy* 24: 354–76.

Panagariya, Arvind. 2009. "Climate Change and India: Implications and Policy Options." Final version (www.columbia.edu/~ap2231/Policy Papers/IPF Panagariya Climate Change final October 1 2009.pdf).

Parikh, Jyoti, and Kirit Parikh. 2009. "Climate Change: A Parking Place Model for a Just Global Compact" (http://policydialogue.org/files/events/Parikh_-_Parking_Place_Model.pdf).

Patel, Urjit R. 2010. "Decarbonisation Strategies: How Much, How, Where and Who Pays For $\Delta \leq 2oC$?" Working paper 39. Brookings (March).

Pauwelyn, Joost. 2009. "Statement of Joost Pauwelyn . . . Testimony before the Subcommittee on Trade of the House Committee on Ways and Means, March 24, 2009" (http://waysandmeans.house.gov/media/pdf/111/pauw.pdf).

Posner, Eric A., and Cass R. Sunstein. 2008. "Justice and Climate Change." Discussion Paper 08-04. Harvard University, Kennedy School of Government.

Posner, Eric, and David Weisbach. 2010. *Climate Change Justice.* Princeton University Press.

Prasad, Eswar, Raghuram G. Rajan, and Arvind Subramanian. 2007. "Foreign Capital and Economic Growth." *Brookings Papers on Economic Activity* 38, no. 1: 153–230.

Prati, Alessandro, and Thierry Tressel. 2006. "Aid Volatility and Dutch Disease: Is There a Role for Macroeconomic Policies?" IMF Working Paper 06/145. Washington: International Monetary Fund.

Rajan, Raghuram G., and Arvind Subramanian. 2008. "Aid and Growth: What Does the Cross-Country Evidence Really Show?" *Review of Economics and Statistics* 90, no. 4: 643–65.

———. 2011. "Aid, Dutch Disease and Manufacturing Growth." *Journal of Development Economics* 94, no. 1: 106–18.

Rodrik, Dani. 2009. "The Real Exchange Rate and Economic Growth." *Brookings Papers on Economic Activity* 39, no. 2: 365–439.

Rogoff, Kenneth, M. Ayhan Kose, Eswar Prasad, and Shang-Jin Wei. 2004. "Effects of Financial Globalization on Developing Countries: Some Empirical Evidence." Occasional Paper 220. Washington: International Monetary Fund (May).

Saran, Shyam. 2009. "Global Governance and Climate Change." *Global Governance: A Review of Multilateralism and International Institutions* 15 no. 4: 457–60.

Spence, Michael. 2009. "Climate Change, Mitigation and Developing Country Growth." PowerPoint presentation. New Delhi: Indian Council for Research and International Economic Relations (http://icrier.org/pdf/Presentation7sep09.pdf).

Stern, Nicholas Herbert. 2007. *The Economics of Global Climate Change: The Stern Review.* Cambridge University Press.

———. 2009a. "Climate Change, Internationalism and India in the 21st Century." Jawaharlal Nehru Memorial Lecture, Chatham House, London, July 15, 2009 (www2.lse.ac.uk/GranthamInstitute/publications/Policy/docs/PPIntandIndiaStern July09.pdf).

———. 2009b. *The Global Deal: Climate Change and the Creation of a New Era of Progress and Prosperity.* New York: PublicAffairs.

———. 2009c. "Transatlantic Perspective on Climate Change and Trade Policy." Keynote address at workshop sponsored by the Peterson Institute for International Economics and the World Resources Institute, Washington, March 4.

Strand, Jon. 2009. "Revenue Management Effects Related to Financial Flows Generated by Climate Policy." World Bank Policy Research Paper 5053. Washington: World Bank.

Subramanian, Arvind. 2011. *Eclipse: Living in the Shadow of China's Economic Dominance*. Washington: Peterson Institute for International Economics.

Tamiotti, Ludivine, Robert The, Vesile Kulaçoğlu, Anne Olhoff, Benjamin Simmons, and Hussein Abaza. 2009. *Trade and Climate Change: A Report by the United Nations Environment Programme and the World Trade Organization*. Geneva: WTO Publications, June.

United Nations Development Program. 2007. *Human Development Report 2007/2008: Fighting Climate Change—Human Solidarity in a Divided World*. New York: Palgrave Macmillan.

Wheeler, David. 2010. "The Economics of Population Policy for Carbon Emissions Reduction in Developing Countries." CGD Working Paper 229. Washington: Center for Global Development.

Wheeler, David, and Saurabh Shome. 2009. "Less Smoke, More Mirrors: Where India Really Stands on Solar Power and Other Renewables." CGD Working Paper 204. Washington: Center for Global Development.

Wheeler, David, and Kevin Ummel. 2007. "Another Inconvenient Truth: A Carbon-Intensive South Faces Environmental Disaster, No Matter What the North Does." CGD Working Paper 134. Washington: Center for Global Development.

Winkler, Harald. 2010. "An Architecture for Long-Term Climate Change: North-South Cooperation Based on Equity and Common but Differentiated Responsibilities." In *Global Climate Governance beyond 2012: Architecture, Agency and Adaptation,* edited by Frank Biermann, Philipp Pattberg, and Fariborz Zelli. Cambridge University Press.

Winkler, Harald, Bernd Brouns, and Sivan Kartha. 2006. "Future Mitigation Commitments: Differentiating among Non-Annex I Countries." *Climate Policy* 5: 469–86.

World Bank. 2009. *World Development Report 2010: Development and Climate Change*. Washington: World Bank.

World Trade Organization. 1987. "United States: Taxes on Petroleum and Certain Imported Substances—Report of the Panel, Adopted on 17 June 1987 (L/6175–34S/136)" (http://www.wto.org/english/tratop_e/dispu_e/87superf.pdf).

# Index

# The Center for Global Development

The Center for Global Development works to reduce global poverty and inequality through rigorous research and active engagement with the policy community to make the world a more prosperous, just, and safe place for us all. The policies and practices of the rich and the powerful—in rich nations, as well as in the emerging powers, international institutions, and global corporations—have significant impacts on the world's poor people. We aim to improve these policies and practices through research and policy engagement to expand opportunities, reduce inequalities, and improve lives everywhere. By pairing research with action, CGD goes beyond contributing to knowledge about development. We conceive of and advocate for practical policy innovations in areas such as trade, aid, health, education, climate change, labor mobility, private investment, access to finance, and global governance to foster shared prosperity in an increasingly interdependent world.